Listening to Handel

Unlocking the Masters Series, No. 30

Series Editor: Robert Levine

Listening
to Handel
An Owner's Manual

David Hurwitz

ab

AMADEUS
PRESS

Lanham • Boulder • New York • London

Published by Amadeus Press
An imprint of The Rowman & Littlefield Publishing Group, Inc.
4501 Forbes Boulevard, Suite 200, Lanham, Maryland 20706
www.rowman.com

6 Tinworth Street, London SE11 5AL, United Kingdom

Book design and composition by Snow Creative

Library of Congress Cataloging-in-Publication Data is available upon request.

ISBN: 978-1-57467-487-3

∞™ The paper used in this publication meets the minimum requirements of American National Standard for Information Sciences—Permanence of Paper for Printed Library Materials, ANSI/NISO Z39.48-1992.

Printed in the United States of America

To Sylvia Kahan

Contents

Preface

Handel was one of the most prolific of all the great composers. Indeed, it's sometimes said that he wrote more notes than anyone before or since, although I have no idea who possibly could do the homework necessary to support that claim. Let's just say that he wrote a lot, and leave it at that. What this means, pragmatically, is that the opportunities for listening are vast and, happily, varied. As a subject of scholarship Handel requires and rewards a lifetime of dedication and specialization, but you don't have to make that kind of commitment to have a terrific listening experience, or enrich your record collection. I like plenty of other music just as well, and I suspect that you do too.

For many years, after singing in countless performances of *Messiah* at annual Christmas concerts and then playing timpani in the orchestra, I felt bored with Handel. This was because I didn't really know him, but also because no one gave me a reason to find out what I might have been missing. This situation changed a few decades ago, thanks to a friendship with a very good musician, the late conductor Antonio de Almeida, who had a real Handel fetish for exactly the right reason: because the music was tremendous fun and there was so much of it to discover. The idea that listening to Handel could be an exploration of the new, instead of the "same old, same old," took me completely by surprise.

Since then, I have spent countless very enjoyable hours over several decades listening to the widest range of Handel's output, both in my professional capacity as a critic and journalist as well as for personal pleasure, and this book offers the results of that particular journey. If you are only passingly familiar with Handel and are looking for a guide to his music generally, you should find the following pages helpful. I also suspect that even those who know Handel pretty well will welcome the chance to listen with fresh ears, and perhaps make some new discoveries in the process. For, while there are many excellent studies of Handel and his music, few focus on the act of listening, strategies for exploring his vast legacy, and the availability of recordings for enjoyment at home. Besides, when it comes to Handel, there are *always* new discoveries.

This book contains information of three basic types: general surveys of large chunks of Handel's output; more detailed discussions of specific works; and essays about musical issues of special interest (specifically, Handel's habit of borrowing and his methods of musical characterization). There will be, inevitably, plenty of overlap, which I think is a good thing. The works selected for detailed discussion are not necessarily his most famous, but they are some of his most distinctive and enjoyable. I chose this approach because it offers an especially diverse and absorbing listening adventure, with as many avenues as possible into this enormous and very distinctive musical universe. At the beginning or end of each chapter you will also find discographies of recommended recordings for potential collectors, where these have not already been mentioned in the main text.[1]

Indeed, in the discussion that follows, I will be mentioning a lot of recordings, because the reality today is that this is how most listeners will get to know Handel's music, especially the less familiar items—and it's a great way to do it. Most Handel studies and biographies, even by the greatest scholars, such as England's Winton Dean, are compromised by the fact that until the past decade or two it was impossible to hear first-class interpretations of vast quantities of Handel's music. Operas were not staged, oratorios remained unsung, and as for the early cantatas and serenatas—well, they might as well not have existed.

Fortunately all of that has changed thanks to the modern record industry, but only quite recently. The reason for this is that the glut of classical recordings of the basic repertoire that overwhelmed the marketplace in the 1980s and '90s forced artists to look farther afield for new projects. Unknown works by great composers offer particularly fertile ground for exploration, and no great composer has left us more unknown work than Handel. You can say what you will about any piece of music based on study of the score, but the truth is that until you have heard it played, and played well, you don't know it. If we are talking about anything beyond the keyboard or chamber music repertoire, this usually means listening to recordings. You will find here everything you need to build a Handel discography in as much depth as you choose.

So, while there is no need to read this book in chapter order, I do suggest that you start with the introduction, and above all spend some time listening to the accompanying samples. All come from highly recommendable releases on the Harmonia Mundi label, and all will be discussed thoroughly in the chapters that follow. I will also offer many other suggestions for building a Handel discography, but there's no need to wait. Just dive in.

In adopting this purely practical approach, I hope to show you just how much fun listening to Handel, even (or especially) unfamiliar Handel, can be. I will only include as much biography as helps to provide useful background, because when I say that his works are "fun," I really mean it. Classical music is supposed to be many things: beautiful, of course, culturally significant, edifying, sophisticated, and all the rest, but to call it merely "entertaining" risks sounding demeaning, and "fun" is downright insulting. Never mind that even *Messiah*, in Handel's day, was called an "entertainment." The bottom line is that Handel's music possesses all of those higher qualities while still being great fun to listen to, and it really doesn't matter what he was writing about—whether the music is vocal or instrumental, happy or sad, secular or sacred.

In other words, the fun is innate, and a major component of Handel's expressive authenticity. Consider, for example, Cleopatra's celebratory aria "Da tempeste il legno infranto" ("As the ship, broken by storms") from the opera *Giulio Cesare*. It's included among the sample tracks. The words compare Cleopatra's confidence of ultimate victory in love to the sailor's relief when a storm-tossed ship finally arrives safely into port. Don't worry about the text in detail; that's what it says, and for now it's all you need to know. Go ahead. Give it a listen.

This is what's called a "simile" aria in the baroque opera business, for obvious reasons, and the repertoire is full of them. Most composers of the period would probably focus on the "stormy" imagery as an excuse to write music full of rushing strings and other forms of instrumental turbulence. Handel, instead, decides to have some fun with his heroine. He writes a dance—a hornpipe, in fact, a sailor's jig. Coming from the exotic and voluptuous Cleopatra, this catchy, earthy, "common" music slyly reminds us that she's just an ordinary gal at heart, and for that reason a real, relatable person despite the stylized trappings of the operatic medium.

Shortly after Handel's death and for much of the nineteenth and twentieth centuries, the opportunity to appreciate this aspect of his art, as well as the sheer sensual pleasure that listening to his music affords, was buried under a pall of Victorian sanctimoniousness. Today, it risks being similarly stifled, although in a different way and for different reasons that we will touch on later, by the (sometimes) dogmatic certitude of academicians and period performance specialists. Few composers beyond Handel have been at once so poorly yet so enthusiastically served by their champions.

Let me give you one brief example. In 1799 the Reverend William Coxe, son of royal physician William Coxe, published a little book called *Anecdotes of George Frederick Handel and John Christopher Smith*. Smith was Handel's copyist and a close friend of Coxe, the father. The account of Handel's life, which is thoroughly superficial, concludes with the words, "He has the highest claim for moral and religious excellence. His pen was never debased to the disgraceful practice of an effeminate or seductive style of composition; it is entitled to the first attribute of praise—it is sublime, affecting, animated, and devoted, without the gloom of superstition, to the service of God."[2]

This statement pretty well summarizes the posthumous popular view of Handel up to and including the present day. It is not entirely absurd. Handel was sincerely religious after his fashion, and more important, deeply moral; his music could be called sublime. Only he could tell us to what extent it was all devoted "to the service of God." Our perception of "effeminacy" as a moral failing or aesthetic crime has changed since Handel's time, and the very notion is extremely problematic and complex as regards musical expression. Suffice it to say that the greatest operatic characters are almost entirely women, and their creators were men. So if we take "effeminacy" to mean "feminine" qualities more generally and not merely "weakness," then Coxe's statement is pure nonsense. Beyond that, if ever there was a composer whose work could and should be called flagrantly and unapologetically "seductive," it is Handel.

More irritatingly, Coxe's view belongs to the "music as castor oil" school of appreciation—something to be listened to as a penance because "it's good for you." Classical music, especially, has always availed itself of this particular bit of PR foolishness due to the simple fact that it still works in promoting the product; and the reason it works is that full enjoyment requires a larger investment of leisure time in mere listening than most of us feel comfortable making. It's a guilty pleasure. So we look for a justification beyond merely having fun. Isn't that sad? And what a distorted view of Handel has developed as a result!

The real Handel has always been bigger—much bigger—than any of the niches into which later commentators have tried to place him. His music embraces an entire cosmos of color, texture, melody, harmony, and expression. Its heights are dizzying, its depths fathomless, its warmth and humanity boundless. His talent was Shakespearian in its range. He rewards performers and listeners alike as do few others. Doing him full justice is impossible, and would require a book of much greater length than any yet written. Still, as I'm sure you will agree, there's plenty to be gained just by taking the first steps. So, get ready to do lots more listening, and let the fun—or entertainment—begin.

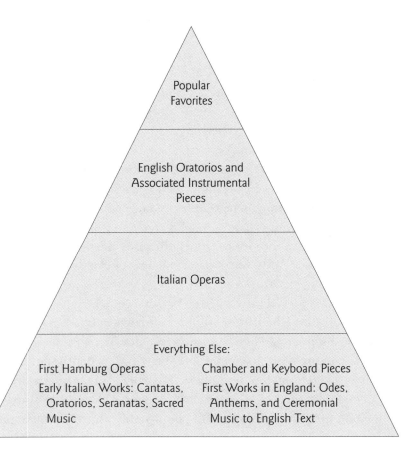

Introduction

Listening to the Mysterious Mr. Handel

S tart with the music. Handel's *Ode for the Birthday of Queen Anne* was composed in 1713. It is not likely that Her Majesty ever heard it, nor is it one of his more popular or important works. No matter. The opening number, for countertenor (male alto), trumpet, and strings must be ranked among the most heavenly effusions of melody in Handel's output. Here is the text:

> Eternal source of light divine,
> With double warmth thy beams display,
> And with distinguish'd glory shine,
> To add a lustre to this day.

Take a moment and listen before reading further.

Lasting only about three minutes, this duet for intertwining trumpet and voice, accompanied by soft string chords, not only perfectly illustrates and embodies the words; it tells us something very useful and interesting about its composer. Specifically, it draws our attention to Handel's sensitivity to timbre and texture, both instrumental and vocal. His use of the trumpet as a lyrical instrument imitating the voice, for example, is unusual in this context. Operatic arias for trumpet and voice were common in Handel's day, and he wrote more than his share of them. Most, however, are heroic in tone, celebrating the instrument's iconic presence as the symbol of victory in military music. In those pieces, the voice often imitates the trumpet's fanfares and characteristic battle signals.

Here, however, Handel does just the opposite. The trumpet sings. Mingled with the unearthly timbre of the countertenor's vocal range, the result really does evoke the luminous, timeless, tranquil glory of the divine light mentioned in the text. It is an effect achieved through the simplest of means, but it reveals the composer's incredibly sophisticated ear; his understanding of how to use instrumental and vocal color—even the odd vocal color of the male alto—to get exactly the effects he desires. In this respect Handel was unique in his time. He was music's first great master of scoring.

Next we turn to an earlier work, the psalm setting Dixit Dominus of 1707. A year earlier Handel had left Germany to study and gain practical experience in Italy, the "land of music" and the place where many aspiring composers went to earn their professional credentials. Already a well-trained musician and a keyboard virtuoso of astonishing accomplishment, he wound up eventually in Rome where his first love, opera, was forbidden by papal decree. Most of his Roman compositions, then, were composed for private or church performance, including this one.

Widely regarded as Handel's first masterpiece, Dixit Dominus is an expansive setting of the 110th Psalm (109th in the Vulgate numbering). The text may surprise listeners whose experience of the psalms consists of the most popular ones—those along the lines of "Praise the Lord" or "The Lord is my shepherd," and that sort of thing. This one speaks of the defeat of God's enemies in the most brutal and graphic terms; it is normally recited as part of the Catholic Vespers (evening) service, and settings were very popular among baroque composers of Handel's day, possibly because of its terrifyingly vivid imagery.

Handel's setting, for its time and purpose, is lavishly scored: five soloists (two sopranos, alto, tenor, and bass), five-part chorus, strings with divided violins and violas, plus a *basso continuo* consisting of cellos, basses, organ, and possibly also a harpsichord. The vocal writing is brilliant and technically challenging for both soloists and choir. Handel clearly wished to impress his patrons, but his boldness of conception and the bigness of scale remain fundamental stylistic traits no matter what the period. The two numbers offered here follow one another consecutively and set the following grim but juicy Latin text (followed by the King James Bible translation):

1. Dominus a dextris tuis; confregit in die irae suae reges.
2a. Judicabit in nationibus; implebit ruinas;
2b. conquassabit capita in terra multorum.

The Lord at thy right hand shall strike through kings in the day
of his wrath.
He shall judge among the heathen, he shall fill the places with
the dead bodies;
He shall wound the heads over many countries.

The first part, "Dominus a dextris tuis," begins with agitated violin
figures over a relentless, rapid bass line. Handel gives the initial exposi-
tion of the text to the soloists from the top down: first, the sopranos
leading to an elaborate continuation for the solo bass. Then the full
chorus enters with a variation of the same music accompanied by the
full string section, while the bass line keeps up its energetic motion
down below. It's a short piece, only a couple of minutes long, but admirably effective in suggesting the irresistible inevitability of divine wrath.

For his next movement, Handel writes a brief double fugue—that is,
each clause has its own distinctive melody, with the individual themes
presented consecutively in staggered entries by the chorus, after which
Handel combines them. The punishment thus arises musically out of the
initial act of judgment. For the line "He shall judge among the heathen,"
Handel offers an aptly solemn chorale in long, flowing notes. Then the
strings take off in rapid motion as the singers relish the thought of the
dead bodies' piling up. Note especially the graphic falling figures and
pauses ricocheting from voice to voice at the words "implebit ruinas."
You get the picture whether you understand the Latin or not.

Now comes the shocker. As the head bashing begins with "conquassabit capita in terra multorum," Handel writes a war march based on
the hard sounds of the individual syllables in the word "conquassabit."
The music has a barbaric impact produced by stretching out the "ah"
vowel in heavily accented, block chords: "con-qua-ssa-a-a-a-a-a-bit."
What we actually hear is more of a primal grunt than human language;
it is extraordinary, frightening, and let's not forget that this music was
intended for liturgical performance, in a church. Less prayerful sounds
it would be difficult to imagine.

The truth is that no matter what he was writing, Handel was a
composer for the theater first and foremost. His music is invariably
dramatic. In some respects this was not unique. All composers of the
period enjoyed using tones to illustrate their texts. It was common

practice then and now. Nevertheless, it's probably safe to say that no setting of the Dixit Dominus matches this one in take-no-prisoners impact and immediacy. Handel's contemporaries evidently agreed. His music sounded fresh and new. Its expressive intensity took Rome by storm right from the start.

The very next year, in 1708, Handel was ready to give his Roman fans an even bigger taste of what he could do. His sacred oratorio *La Resurrezione* ("The Resurrection") answers the musical question, "What're a bored aristocrat and his fifteen hundred (or so) friends to do for entertainment on Easter Sunday when just about everything enjoyable is strictly forbidden?" The answer, obviously, was to hire the hottest new composer in town to write a custom-tailored work to be produced technically "in concert," but with full theatrical backdrops, a huge orchestra of more than forty players led by none other than Arcangelo Corelli (the greatest Italian instrumental music composer of the day), and a first-class roster of singers—including even, blasphemously, a real woman rather than a castrato as Mary Magdalene. The fact that Handel's patron Francesco Ruspoli got reprimanded by the pope for his audacity points to the success of the whole scandalous enterprise.

The Dixit Dominus reveals that Handel was a very great master—indeed *the* very greatest master—of choral writing from the very start of his career. However, listeners familiar with the famous English oratorio choruses and the Coronation Anthems will not find anything like them in these early Italian pieces. As in opera of the same period, the chief medium of expression is the solo, and specifically the so-called da capo aria. We will discuss these in greater detail shortly, but for now suffice it to say that *da capo* means "from the top" and represents a song in ABA form. Handel wrote literally thousands of them, and naturally the devil is in the details.

La Resurrezione, which has been revived with great success recently both live and on recordings, doesn't have much of a plot. A bunch of biblical characters stand around and talk about salvation and the like, but that's not really the point. The music is what matters, and it is stunning. There's a brief overture, and then Handel opens with an absolute showstopper of an aria, "Open, O gates of Hell," sung by an angel of the Lord (to which Lucifer responds grumpily, "Close those damn gates!"

or poetic words to that effect). Here is the text of the aria, which is led off by jubilant trumpets, oboes, and strings.

> ANGEL:
> (A) Disseratevi, oh porte d'Averno,
> e al bel lume d'un lume ch'è eterno tutto in lampi si sciolga
> l'orror!
> (B) Cedete, horride porte,
> cedete al re di gloria
> che della sua vittoria
> voi siete il primo onor.
> (A) repeated
>
> (A) Be unbarred, O gates of Hell,
> and let the beautiful radiance of a light that shines eternally melt
> away the horror!
> (B) Give way, dreadful gates,
> Give way to the King of Glory,
> So that in His victory
> You gain the first honor.
> (A) repeated, with ornamentation

I have indicated for convenience which words belong to the "A" and "B" sections, respectively. After "B," the "A" bit gets repeated with ornamentation added by the singer. The vocal writing, even without the improvised embellishments, is insanely virtuosic, and pure opera. While the actual plot of the oratorio and the circumstances of its performance precluded dramatic presentation, both the music itself and its placement as the work's curtain-raiser represent a telling instance of Handelian theatrics. This aria has become quite popular as a separate item in recitals by sopranos with a superb coloratura technique, unlimited breath control, and an acute sense of danger. In addition to the amazing Lucy Crowe on the accompanying recording, Sandrine Piau and Julia Lezhneva, among others, have sung this music on disc with dazzling success.

If you have a look at Handel's musical "food" pyramid at the start of this chapter, you will note that all three of the pieces in this initial tasting come from the very bottom—from the vast "everything else" category of early works. They were composed in the six-year period between 1707 and 1713; that is, when Handel was between twenty-two and twenty-eight years old. The exceptional quality of the results being incontestable, the only conclusion we can draw is that Handel was a first-rate genius virtually from day one. He did not spend the first fifty-six years of his life noodling around to no particular purpose before waking up in 1741 and writing *Messiah*. This fact in turn raises the first question that justifies the word "mysterious" in the title of this introduction. How did so much great music come to be neglected for so long?

There is no single answer to this question. Rather, a complex web of factors conspired to draw a veil of silence over Handel's output. The first of these is our own ignorance about the man. For a composer this famous, we know very little about him. Sure, we get the basics: that he was born in 1685 in Halle, Germany, into a decently middle class family. He received a good musical education, played violin and keyboard in the Hamburg opera, went to Italy in 1706 for additional training, and made a first trip to London in 1710 before settling there permanently two years later. To the extent the music survives, we usually know what Handel wrote and often for whom—fortunately, he was pretty tidy in this respect. We also know a great deal about the musical life of the places in which he lived, and the circumstances under which his works were played.

But about the man himself we have practically nothing. He never married. He left no children to speak or write about him posthumously. He taught no students of any significance (although he did teach), and took part in no serious controversies. He was a glutton with a short temper. He hired the best people, paid them well, and demanded superior performance. Especially for the period, he was incredibly honest and decent when it came to business affairs and his handling of money. Few of his letters have survived, and virtually none of musical interest. Handel kept his private life private, leaving us almost completely in the dark concerning his views on music, the practice of composition, his artistic ideals—in short, just about anything that would cast a light onto his aesthetics, working habits, and the rationale behind the decisions that he made. It is all, as I say, a near total mystery, albeit a very fascinating one.

The second major factor in creating the "Handel mystery" is historical: his music, and baroque music generally, went out of fashion during the last few decades of the eighteenth century, and only started to be reconsidered in the middle of the twentieth. There was no such thing as "classical music" in Handel's day; indeed, the very idea only evolved gradually during the 1800s in connection with the rise of the middle classes as arts consumers, and the consequent founding of municipal orchestras, opera companies, and other institutions destined to gratify the public taste for high-end entertainment. Before that, *music* meant "contemporary music," usually tailored to suit aristocratic or ecclesiastical taste, and all the rest was simply old news.

Much is made of the Bach revival begun by Felix Mendelssohn in 1829, as well as the publication of complete editions of Bach and Handel (and other early masters) by the close of that century; but in the days before modern broadcast and recording technology, these efforts, historically significant though they may have been, remained largely of local or musicological interest. Handel was principally a composer of Italian *opera seria* ("serious opera"). He wrote more than forty of them. Staging an opera is extremely complicated, expensive, and wholly dependent on the availability of singers willing to undertake the major roles. So it should come as no surprise to learn that after Handel's last opera, *Deidamia*, was produced in 1741, nearly two hundred years would pass until a tentative revival of this vast corpus began.

Those works of Handel that might be heard during the long night of neglect, *Messiah* and a couple more oratorios, the Coronation Anthems, *Water Music, Royal Fireworks Music*, and a few others, had to be updated to suit modern taste. This process began with Mozart, who produced new orchestrations of several Handel masterpieces, including *Messiah, Acis and Galatea, Ode for St. Cecilia's Day*, and *Alexander's Feast*. Although well made and euphonious to a fault, these arrangements are already far from the originals, and they render the music curiously inert by softening its sharper sonic contours. In England during the nineteenth century, Handel became the ultimate "festival" composer, his music to be performed by huge choirs and orchestras that necessitated increasingly ponderous tempos. The result was undoubtedly overwhelming in spots, but little else.

During his lifetime Handel became an English institution, and this fact constitutes the third (and final) part of this particular musical mystery. He was the first great national composer. His Coronation Anthem *Zadok the Priest* has been sung at the anointing of every British monarch since 1727. He was so good at creating "public" music that after his death these works swamped everything else, and the pieces that were not intended for epic mass celebrations (such as *Messiah*) were enlarged and adapted to fit them. Handel was perfectly aware of his strengths and his value in this respect. After all, he did ask to be buried in Westminster Abbey, and he got his wish. Statues were erected in his image. He became a monument.

This was a mixed blessing. On the one hand, certain of his works that fit this nationalist public perception survived his passing. On the other hand, monuments don't need to be discovered, catalogued, or even listened to with particular care. They exist to be acknowledged, admired as impressive objects and, having received their due, are largely taken for granted. So it proceeded with Handel's reputation in England. He was (it was assumed) a known quantity, part of the ordinary cultural background. Nothing else explains the curious fact that no English publisher or academic institution ever attempted a critical edition of his complete works. Of only two such projects, one of which is still ongoing, both are German initiatives despite the fact that the primary sources for most of Handel's music reside in England.

There wasn't even a reasonably accurate biography of Handel until 1857, when Victor Schoelcher, a Frenchman living in exile in Britain, published the first ever story of his life and works (in English translation) based on actual examination of primary sources. Schoelcher was shocked to learn, among other things, that no one had examined Handel's manuscripts in generations, that there was no accurate catalog of his works—heck, no one even bothered to get the date of his birth correct. Most people thought, if they thought about it at all, that he was born on February 24, 1684, whereas both Handel himself and the available baptismal records prove incontestably that his birth occurred on February 23, 1685. If even connoisseurs could get this basic fact wrong, you can only imagine what the situation must have been regarding his music.

The gulf between modern Handel scholarship, then, and the public perception of him is vast. Naturally there are many superb Handel scholars in England today. Indeed, that's where most of them are, and no single group of musical professionals has worked harder to broaden awareness of his achievement; but the audience for their work remains small in the face of a monolithic reputation two centuries in the making. For most music consumers, the Handel we know and love is the public Handel, and that is more than enough. I am still astonished that whenever I play pieces to musical friends such as the aria "Disseratevi," just discussed, or perhaps Dejanira's mad scene from *Hercules*, I invariably get the response: "That's amazing. *Handel* wrote that?"

So, these three factors—our lack of knowledge about the man, the march of music history after his death, and Handel's objectification as a national institution—account for much of the mystery that prevents us from seeing him whole. What we might call "less global" or local circumstances comprise the rest. These include, for example, the fact that Handel's early sacred music was written for the Catholic Church whereas Handel was a Lutheran who eventually settled in a Protestant country, that the lead roles in his operas were mostly taken by castratos, and the fact that his English audiences naturally preferred works with texts in that language. In other words, any number of individual considerations, both musical and nonmusical, might conspire to favor one body of his work over another.

The existence of the "Handel mystery" is extremely ironic, because as I hope you've noticed the music itself couldn't be more enjoyable or expressively more direct. Indeed, from his earliest days Handel created a personal style that belies the old saw that most baroque music "sounds the same." He has a number of distinctive musical fingerprints, many of them amazingly simple, that tell us exactly who it is that we're listening to. I will mention many of them in the following chapters, but just to prove the point let me describe one of the most immediately audible: Handel's proprietary endings.

You would be amazed by how many composers have preferred ways of concluding a piece of music, particularly in quick tempos. Finding a convincing ending is always tricky, and so a formula that works is likely to get reused, especially if it helps to put a personal stamp on the last notes that you hear. Sibelius, for example, likes solemn, "amen" chords (finale of Symphony No. 2 or *Finlandia*). Rachmaninov prefers an emphatic "dum, dadadum!" at the end of his Second and Third Piano Concertos, or Second Symphony. Haydn's way of ending a finale with three repeated chords (Symphony No. 88 and other places too numerous to mention) was so characteristic that it has been associated with him ever since, even though it seems the most natural thing in the world.

Handel actually has several personal endings. The first of these is so famous that again, as with Haydn, you would think everyone was doing it—except that before Handel no one seems to have done it to anything like the same extent, and afterward anyone who used it sounded like an imitator. I'm talking about the grand cadence in slow tempo to wrap up a big choral number. You know what I mean: at the end of the "Hallelujah Chorus" there's a big pause, and then choir and orchestra sing a closing flourish in slow tempo, often with trumpets and timpani tossing in a brilliant rhythmic fanfare for added effect. You can hear exactly the same formula in the concluding chorus of the oratorio *Judas Maccabaeus*, "Rejoice, O Judah! Hallelujah! Amen," included in our track listing.

Sometimes the orchestra keeps going while the voices execute the pause, and then everyone comes together for the big adagio (slow) cadence, as at the end of the Coronation Anthem *Zadok the Priest*; but chances are you will hear some version of this ending whenever Handel is in "Hallelujah" mode, as he very often was. That said, he does not restrict himself to vocal music. The overture to the oratorio *Samson* offers a fine example from the orchestral repertoire. Or check out the second movement of the Concerto Grosso Op. 6, No. 1, included on the accompanying CD. Here Handel indicates the pause, but not the adagio tempo, which most conductors do anyway simply because the music seems to imply it. When early music specialist Nikolaus Harnoncourt decided to play this ending strictly in tempo on his recording of the piece, the result sounded positively shocking, sending this music lover scurrying to the score to see what Handel actually wrote.

It's useful to note in this respect that there is a difference between a characteristic and a mannerism—a habit overused. Handel has many other endings to big choral movements, or the works they conclude, and he seems to have chosen among them with great care. One of his other tricks is to finish gently, after a grand climax, with a simple but somehow fulfilling cadence, in tempo, mainly for strings. You can hear this at the end of the opera *Ariodante*, the oratorios *Saul* and *Hercules*, or the choral conclusion to act 2 of *Parnasso in Festa*. The effect is something akin to a safe and soft landing after a long and adventurous flight. Why it works so well I can't say, but it does, and it's entirely typical of Handel's real-life sensitivity to sound. His solutions always produce their intended effect in performance.

For music of an especially light and lively character, particularly solo arias in his operas and oratorios, Handel often employs another type of ending: a sudden downward "snap" in the form of a two-note, falling octave. Perhaps its most famous use in later music occurs at the conclusion of Mahler's First Symphony. You can hear Handel employ it at the end of the "A" section of the aria "Da tempeste il legno infranto" from *Giulio Cesare,* which we have already encountered in the preface. The very suddenness of this two-note gesture only reinforces its finality.

Browsing through some other pieces at random, you can hear this ending in the aria "Se cangio spoglia, non congia core" ("Looks may change, not the heart") in *Serse*, or you can try "Chi possessore è del mio core" ("Who owns my heart") from *Orlando*. In *The Occasional Oratorio* (now there's a work that few have ever heard of), two arias with this ending follow in quick succession: "When warlike ensigns wave on high" and "The sword that's drawn in virtue's cause." If you're a *Messiah* fan, consider the aria "But who may abide the day of His coming" (alto version). These examples offer a very small sample of the dozens of times that Handel chooses to conclude the ritornello (the main theme) of an aria in this manner. I find it remarkable that a gesture so simple can be at once so effective and so distinctive a stylistic signpost.

What we hear in all of these examples is a composer in complete command of his musical vocabulary, right down to the smallest detail. There is a world of difference between those many baroque composers who "all sound the same," using the language of their time with no special ability or insight, and an artist such as Handel, who understands how to use the elements of a common style to create music of uncommon power and accuracy of expression. You might call it the difference between prose on the one hand, and poetry on the other. Both may use the same words, but the latter employs them to more vivid effect. The better you get to know Handel, the more evident this observation becomes, and the more distinctive he sounds.

The principal forms in baroque music are the aria for solo voice, the concerto and suite in orchestral works, and the sonata in chamber pieces for small forces—typically keyboard plus flute(s) or violin(s). Musical texture in all forms depends on the opposition of solo lines on top, with harmonic support concentrated in the *basso continuo*, or "continuo" for short, consisting of low-pitched instruments on the bass line plus a keyboard or plucked stringed instrument—harpsichord, organ, lute, or theorbo—to fill in the chords. The use of counterpoint in the shape of fugues or other multivoiced structures provides added weight and rhetorical emphasis to vocal and instrumental music alike.

Handel along with Bach—and in France, Rameau—carried the baroque style to its apex. By the time Handel died in 1759, music had already moved on to the preclassical language of early Haydn and his contemporaries: composers such as C. P. E. and J. C. Bach, Christoph Willibald Gluck, and the musicians of the Mannheim school. For this reason, both Bach and Handel are sometimes regarded as musical conservatives, composers who consolidated and had the final say on existing norms and means of expression. However, in Handel's case especially, this picture of him tells only part of the story.

It may be true that Handel was not the most formally adventurous composer of his time, but when it comes to matters of instrumental color and timbre he was little short of revolutionary. He brought orchestral writing to new heights, employing regularly numerous instruments in large ensembles that had previously been rare in England, or anywhere else. These included horns, trombones, extra-large timpani, a wide variety of flutes and recorders, clarinets, harp, something called a *violetta marina*, and his famous bell contraption, the carillon. His feeling even for basic string textures was unparalleled, extremely striking in its sonorousness and sensuality, and his writing for massed voices with orchestra, as previously noted, had no peer in his own day or since.

Handel invented the dramatic oratorio, with its theatrical plot (whether biblical or not) and extensive choral participation. This was a

major innovation that had repercussions both positive (Haydn's oratorios *The Creation* and *The Seasons*, Mendelssohn's *Elijah*) and negative
(the countless soggy Victorian choral works that throttled the development of English music for much of the nineteenth century). He was a
master of languages, perhaps not surprisingly, setting texts in Latin,
Italian, French, Spanish (okay, only one cantata), German, and English.
No composer before or since has been more ecumenical, more all-
embracing in his eclecticism, or more enthusiastic and unapologetic in
his borrowing from others.

One last sample from the track list summarizes all of these observa-
tions in just a couple of minutes of music. It is the "symphony," recitative, and chorus, "Welcome, welcome mighty king!" from the oratorio
Saul. Handel evidently borrowed from someone else the tune of the
chorus, or at least part of it, but he scored it with penetrating psychological insight for voices and carillon. Here is the text:

> **Michal** (Recitative)
> Already see the daughters of the land,
> In joyful dance, with instruments of music,
> Come to congratulate your victory.
>
> **Chorus of Israelites**
> Welcome, welcome, mighty king!
> Welcome all who conquer bring!
> Welcome David, warlike boy,
> Author of our present joy!
> Saul, who hast thy thousands slain,
> Welcome to thy friends again!
> David his ten thousands slew,
> Ten thousand praises are his due!

This chorus incites Saul's jealousy. The jangling timbre of the carillon and use of high-pitched voices sets the mood of jubilation, but its
relentless brightness also jabs at Saul's clouded mind like the maddening
buzz of an insect or the poking of a needle. The notes themselves may
be generic: this is "bell music" that could have come from any period
or any composer. Indeed, it sounds quite similar to "The Viennese

Musical Clock" from the *Háry János* Suite by Hungarian composer Zoltán Kodály, written some two centuries later. If Handel found this music kicking around in some dusty baroque corner, heaven only knows who wrote it in the first instance. What really matters is that the use to which Handel puts his material, whether original or not, is unique to this context, both in sonority and expressive purpose.

Ultimately, all great composers find ways to personalize their musical language, and Handel is no exception. Originality comes in many forms. Some composers place a premium on creating new material; others display great ingenuity in its treatment. Some are masters of counterpoint; others stress harmony, or rhythm. Most of the really great ones do a little bit of everything, and it's the combination of ingredients that varies from one to another. The key is finding a recipe that works. Handel did just that. His methods were as proprietary as the results they produced. They constitute perhaps the greatest mystery of all: the mystery of genius. Fortunately for us, this last mystery is as easy and enjoyable to hear as it is impossible to define. The following chapters explore Handel's genius in greater depth, and will guide you through the myriad treasures that it produced.

The Curse of The Harmonious Blacksmith

(Too?) Popular Favorites

The Harmonious Blacksmith
"Largo" from *Xerxes* (*Serse*)
Water Music
Music for the Royal Fireworks
Zadok the Priest
Messiah

There are basically three types of classical music consumers: the general public, casual listeners, and hard-core aficionados. The works in this chapter made the list because they fit into the middle tier: Handel for people who like classical music but who don't have the time or inclination to make too major a commitment. For such a prolific composer, Handel actually has done pretty well. The above pieces include major works, fully representative of important aspects of his art. He has never really been seen as a "one-shot wonder" along the lines of equally productive colleagues, such as Vivaldi (*The Four Seasons*), Boccherini (Minuet), Albinoni (Adagio), Pachelbel (Canon), C. P. E. Bach (Solfeggio), and so many others. If you own recordings of these Handel selections, you will have made a good start.

That said, there is a twofold danger to taking the "greatest hits" approach. First, it's a mistake to think "most popular" equals "best" or, more pertinently, "only." Nothing could be further from the truth, however splendid these works may be. The rest of this book intends to dispel that pernicious notion. Second, you may not especially like some or all of this music, and therefore decide that Handel just isn't your cup of tea. That was the situation in which I found myself early in my encounters with him—I was more turned on by other pieces (*Saul*, the Dixit Dominus, the Dettingen Te Deum, *Israel in Egypt*, *Semele*), and only came around to the more obvious choices somewhat later, once I felt comfortable with Handel's language and style. With the understanding that every listener's personal feelings, positive or negative, are perfectly valid, let's take a closer look at these iconic works.

The Harmonious Blacksmith (1720)

The Harmonious Blacksmith is a keyboard piece consisting of an extremely catchy tune followed by five increasingly elaborate variations. It represents the fourth and final movement of his Fifth Keyboard Suite in E Major. In Handel's day it would have been performed on a harpsichord, although nowadays you might also hear it in piano recitals. No one knows exactly when Handel wrote it, or how it acquired a title that makes no sense whatsoever. There are various apocryphal stories that need not concern us. It was published in 1720, in an edition supervised by the composer himself. This was unusual. Lots of Handel's music was assembled and disseminated by unscrupulous publishers both in England and abroad. Some of his keyboard pieces, however, turned out to be so popular that he decided to publish them in an authorized edition so as to profit from his own work.

This collection has come down to us as the Eight Great Suites for keyboard. It was followed by additional publications in which Handel took no part, and to this day it is still unclear just how much keyboard music he wrote—let's just say that there is a lot of it. In the catalog of Handel's works most commonly in use, known as the *Händel Werkverzeichnis* (HWV for short), the keyboard music begins with HWV 426, and ends at HWV 612. You do the math. The most recent "complete" set of harpsichord music, which isn't really, was issued by Brilliant Classics and contains nine discs' worth of music. In addition to the suites, of which there may be around a couple dozen in total, there are marvelous individual pieces, including some splendid keyboard arrangements of opera overtures and theatrical music.

The fact that the best-known keyboard collection gets called "great" certainly does not mean that the rest is "lousy" or "not that great." Nevertheless, Handel was not a composer for the keyboard on the level of his exact contemporaries, J. S. Bach and Domenico Scarlatti. The reason for this is simple: both made teaching a major focus of their careers. Bach's students famously included his own children, while Scarlatti worked for Spanish royalty; and so they wrote sophisticated keyboard music as much for instructional as for artistic purposes. Bach, in particular, whose pedagogical leanings were legendary, famously called his greatest collection of such works *Clavier-Übung*, or "Keyboard Practice."

Handel taught students also, if perhaps reluctantly, or as a necessary cost of aristocratic patronage. The amount of keyboard music that he wrote attests to that, and teaching earned easy income that few composers could afford to disdain—especially when starting their careers or if just arrived in new territory. Indeed, the common term for individual keyboard pieces in English was "lesson," but we know practically nothing about Handel's pupils beyond the fact that they existed, never mind his instructional methods; and aside from that single collection of 1720, he never again bothered to organize his own keyboard or pedagogical output for posterity. The result, then, remains a bit of a mess that is still in the process of being sorted out by the scholarly community. We can only wish them luck.

The reason *The Harmonious Blacksmith* has become so popular is simple to understand: it has a tune that you can't get out of your head once you've heard it, and the ensuing variations are extremely easy and fun to follow. The theme falls into two halves, both repeated: AABB. Some players take the opportunity to ornament the repeats, as likely would have been done in Handel's day. This practice adds variety and even more flash to what is already an extremely dazzling piece of keyboard writing.

Although effective on the piano, the piece works best on the harp-sichord because that instrument operates on the dynamic principal of accretion: the more notes that get played, the louder the music sounds. As Handel stuffs each variation with shorter (and therefore quicker) notes, over about four minutes of playing time we hear a natural cre-scendo as brilliant and exciting as it is inexorable. Once again we marvel at Handel's sensitivity to instrumental timbre and sonority, a quality that is characteristic of all of his keyboard music.

That said, *The Harmonious Blacksmith* is just one of four movements. A typical baroque suite starts with a prelude or overture, and then fol-lows it up with four standard dances (allemande, courante, sarabande, and gigue), and any number of extras as desired. In the Eight Great Suites, Handel follows this format, maybe, once—in the marvelous Suite No. 4 in E Minor. I say "maybe" because this piece starts with a movement simply called Allegro, but it does precede the four iconic dances. So this is as close to regularity as Handel gets. Here is the layout for each of the eight suites in the set:

- No. 1: Prélude, Allemande, Courante, Gigue
- No. 2: Adagio, Allegro, Adagio, Allegro
- No. 3: Prélude, Allegro, Allemande, Courante
- No. 4: Allegro, Allemande, Courante, Sarabande, Gigue
- No. 5: Prélude, Allemande, Courante, Air and Variations (later, "The Harmonious Blacksmith")
- No. 6: Prélude, Largo, Allegro, Gigue
- No. 7: Ouverture, Andante, Allegro, Sarabande, Gigue, Passacaille
- No. 8: Prélude, Allegro, Allemande, Courante, Gigue

As you can see, no two suites have exactly the same organization, eloquent testimony to Handel's freedom of form and undogmatic atti-tude toward standard practice. In these days of discographic complete-ness, the best way to find *The Harmonious Blacksmith* may be simply to bite the bullet and get the full set of the Eight Great Suites. That will give you two discs worth of music, and trust me, it won't be a penance. There's a much greater chance that you'll enjoy the rest of the suites, including the remaining movements in No. 5, far more than the miscel-laneous bits on any "Harpsichord Highlights" collection.

Largo from *Xerxes* (*Serse*) (1738)

"Handel's Largo," as it was called back in the day, actually refers to any instrumental arrangement for any forces—but usually string orchestra—of the opening aria "Ombra mai fu" from the opera *Serse* (*Xerxes* in English). First produced in 1738, the work itself was a flop, and like all of Handel's operas it vanished from the stage for nearly two centuries before its first modern revival in the 1920s in Germany. Since then, it has become one of his most frequently offered works in the form.

It may surprise you to learn that this opera, Handel's fortieth, is a comedy. Humor in music is possibly the most misunderstood and undervalued of all possible expressive qualities, and even modern commentators often refer to the work as a serious opera with "comic elements" so as not to suggest that the piece is somehow of lesser quality or importance. Besides humor, the most controversial expressive element in music has got to be sex, and this opera has plenty of that too. Naturally it was doomed.

Handel called his Largo, actually marked "Larghetto" (not quite as slow as Largo) an "Arioso," which is his term for a song consisting only of the "A" section of what would otherwise be the usual, ABA aria form. In other words this short piece, lasting a bit more than three minutes, consists of a single, gorgeous, lyrical melody sung by the castrato lead (today a female alto or male countertenor), introduced by the string orchestra. You can hear it marvelously performed by Andreas Scholl included among the sample tracks. The text consists of a single sentence, and as you can see and hear, this has got to be the most beautiful love song ever addressed—to a tree:

> Ombra mai fu
> di vegetabile,
> cara ed amabile,
> soave più.

> Never was the shade
> of a plant,
> dear and lovely,
> more sweet.

If we want to get species specific, it's a plane tree according to the libretto, and the humor lies in the fact that the music is perfectly serious. Only the words reveal the absurdity of a situation in which Xerxes, the king, evidently has stronger feelings for his favorite fern than for his nominal fiancée, Amastre, who spends most of the opera disguised as a man so as to watch him chase after his brother's girlfriend, Romilda. It all gets resolved in the end and everyone gets married except, of course, the plane tree. With the text broken up into four short lines, as here, you can see the rhyme scheme in the Italian original.

Because the music is so beautiful all by itself, noble and expressive in a way that had a vast impact on English composers right up through Elgar in the twentieth century, the piece works perfectly well divorced from its original context. It became a staple of "pops" programs and a repertoire standard for string orchestras. It also makes a lovely encore number. I do however find it deliciously ironic that most audiences at symphony concerts right up to the present day listen to this work completely unaware of what the words say—indeed of the fact that this Largo originally had words at all.

During the Victorian and Edwardian periods, when humor in so-called serious music was frowned upon in the strongest possible terms, the text of this aria was translated, or should I say, "adapted," into English. Noting that the original Italian words were far too trivial and silly to be wasted on one of Handel's best melodies, in 1905 a certain Nathan Haskell Dole, aided and abetted by noted Handelian pedagogue Ebenezer Prout, came up with this new and improved poetic masterpiece, whose excruciating eloquence speaks for itself:

> Never was hour,
> So fit for festival!
> Brightest and best of all
> Summer's full flow'r!
> Nature's kind pow'r,
> Her prodigality
> Makes the reality
> Love's richest dow'r.

Think that was the last indignity inflicted on this classic example of Handel's pagan sensuality?

Think again.

At some point, this piece was arranged as an anthem entitled "Holy art Thou" by English music publisher Alfred William Phillips (1844– 1936), thus ratifying the evolution of Handel from operatic genius to purveyor of Victorian religious kitsch. At least Phillips had the sense to publish his arrangement under a pseudonym: Leigh Kingsmill. In this version the work has become popular in churches everywhere, and you can hear it very beautifully sung, I must admit, on the Mormon Tabernacle Choir's disc "The Great Handel Choruses" (Sony Classical). Never mind that this is most emphatically *not* a Handel chorus, and that it is billed as deriving from "Handel's Largo," thus avoiding any suggestion that the original had different words. At least the anthem's text, which I will not quote, suits its purpose and is less cringe-worthy than "Love's richest dow'r."

Finally, instrumental arrangements of Handel arias became popular well before his death, and neither he (nor his publishers) had any qualms about turning some of his best tunes into orchestral pieces. For example, Cleopatra's haunting aria "Piangerò la sorte mia" ("I will lament my fate"), from *Giulio Cesare*, serves as the source of the fourth movement Adagio in his Concerto Grosso Op. 6, No. 8; and if you're a big *Messiah* fan, you can enjoy the famous chorus "And the glory of the Lord" as the second movement of the Concerto a Due Cori No. 1, HWV 332.[3] In fact, much of the work consists of orchestral arrangements of individual choruses. It seems that Handel anticipated by a couple of centuries the trend of programming "opera without words."

If you're in the market for a recording of the traditional Largo and want a special treat, try to get a superrich, extra-lush performance such as Eugene Ormandy's with the Philadelphia Orchestra on Sony Classical (formerly Columbia). Ormandy stretches the music out to nearly six decadent, luxurious, sensual minutes. Purists will wince, but the romantic and the sexy are genuine, valid elements of Handel's style that routinely get short-changed in so many of today's cooler, brisker, theoretically historically informed performances.

Water Music (1717) and *Music for the Royal Fireworks* (1749)

Although they date from opposite ends of Handel's English career, the *Water Music* and the *Fireworks Music* have many features in common, and so are best considered together. Both scores are big, public works written for very large forces. The *Water Music* has parts for a "flauto dolce piccolo" or descant (high) recorder, flute, two oboes, bassoon, two horns, trumpets, violins (in three parts), violas, cellos, and basses. This might not seem like much, but we know that the original forces in 1717 totaled at least fifty, all crammed onto a barge, which means that each wind part must have required multiple players, with strings in proportion. The *Fireworks Music* is even larger: flutes (in two parts, number unspecified), twenty-four oboes (in three parts), twelve bassoons (in two parts), nine horns, nine trumpets, bass serpent, contrabassoon, three sets of timpani, multiple snare drums, and (optional but desirable) strings. This makes it one of the largest and greatest wind band pieces ever written to this very day, although it is almost never played as Handel originally intended. Getting twenty-four oboes and twelve bassoons together at the same time still poses a serious logistical challenge.

As you can see clearly even before listening to a single note, because both works originally were intended for performance outdoors, Handel's orchestration has some outstanding features. Specifically, strings and continuo instruments such as the harpsichord do not carry well in the open air, and especially not on a barge in the middle of the River Thames (the setting for the first performances of the *Water Music*). Consequently, both works employ an abundance of woodwind and brass instruments, giving them an unusually colorful basic sonority as well as a strikingly flashy level of technical virtuosity. To hear oboes, trumpets, and horns execute rapid passagework more typical of (and comfortable on) strings will always sound like a tour de force, even as mere accompaniment.

Although in modern performances, which mostly take place indoors, a continuo part for harpsichord is often used in the traditional baroque manner, the fact that Handel doesn't require one means that the parts are unusually self-sufficient, harmonically. This, combined with the flexible scoring as regards the number of musicians on each part, means that the music can be adapted readily to a variety of performance situations, including the modern orchestra. Arrangements of the *Fireworks Music* for more manageable indoor ensembles began with the composer himself. Irish conductor Hamilton Harty's (d. 1941) edition of the *Water Music* earned the work—or bits of it at any rate—an honored place in the standard repertoire, and set the stage for its rediscovery in full by the period performance movement. Before considering these two iconic pieces in greater detail, however let's consider the unique sonority of the baroque orchestra more generally.

Aside from the presence of the *basso continuo*, Handel's typical ensemble differed in several ways from the modern forces that we're used to. The classical orchestra as it evolved in the hands of Haydn, Mozart, and their later eighteenth-century contemporaries consisted of a large body of strings, pairs of woodwinds (flutes, oboes, clarinets, bassoons), horns, and trumpets plus timpani, without keyboard continuo. Later, bigger groupings built on this foundation.

Handel's orchestra similarly had as its basis the large mass of strings, but it would be more correct to think about it less as a collection of instruments arranged by characteristic timbre than by *range*, specifically top, middle and bottom, or soprano (top), tenor/alto (middle), and bass (bottom). "Top" instruments included violins, oboes, flutes, trumpets, and (sometimes) horns. The middle, least numerous group, took in the violas and (sometimes) cellos. Bottom, or bass instruments, meant cellos, basses, bassoons and contrabassoons, as well as the left-hand low register of the keyboard continuo.

Dynamics, when they were indicated at all, were "terraced," meaning either loud or soft, although we must never assume that gradual changes in volume or shading were unusual just because composers didn't often write them into the score. What this really means is that volume could be regulated as much as by the number of participants on a single musical line as by how loudly that line was marked to be played. Handel generally expected a larger number of woodwind players than we find in the classical orchestra to balance both the top and bottom strings (scholars say about one oboe to every three or four violins), and so his most characteristic sonority is the relatively astringent sound of massed violins and oboes playing the principal tunes together. This is the dominating timbre in the Ouverture of the *Water Music*, for example. By eliminating the oboes, Handel can create an entirely different ensemble sonority. As we so often find in his work, the result is as effective as it is simple.

The classical orchestra standardized the string section, which remains to this day a five-part grouping consisting of first and second violins, violas, cellos, and basses. This could be further subdivided as the composer demanded, but Handel's organization was much looser. Especially in arias, for example, we frequently encounter all the violins playing in unison. On the other hand, certain numbers in the *Water Music* ask for violins in three separate parts, a layout that Handel employed very often and clearly enjoyed using for its richness of sonority. This sort of writing arises from a way of thinking about music that is essentially contrapuntal—that is, a function of needing to contrast multiple competing melodic lines of roughly equal weight.

In the classical orchestra, the same instruments that may have the tune also take turns providing the harmonic accompaniment, and so the need to balance these variegated textural layers against the main theme became just as important an aspect of effective scoring. Accordingly, details of dynamics, phrasing, and sonority needed to be indicated with greater specificity (and someone to take control over these issues—the conductor—became a new job description). The continuo disappeared, and the basic texture became homophonic: designed around the principal melody plus its accompaniment. So it has remained to this day.

It's important to bear in mind, however, that these tendencies are just that: generalizations rather than rules. We must always make allowance for the right of composers at all periods to write beautiful melodies with simple accompaniments, or movements exploiting contrapuntal textures. It would also be a mistake to assert that Handel's orchestra or his methods were in any way more "primitive" than what came later. Any tool or technique is only as good as the use made of it, and what Handel achieved with the forces and strategies available to him, as already suggested, was as great as anything anyone has done before or since.

The two works under consideration here, then, are typical of their period, with the distinction that they are more tuneful, more colorful, and yes, more fun to listen to, than most other, similar examples of their type. Both are suites consisting of an overture followed by a collection of dances or character pieces. Almost all of Handel's overtures belong to the variety now known as "French." This means an opening slow march in jerky rhythm ("dotted rhythms" in musical terms, due to notational conventions) followed by a quick section in "learned" style featuring contrapuntal, and specifically fugal, textures. The march may return at the end by way of conclusion, or it can alternate with the allegro, as it does in the *Fireworks Music*, but beyond the basic opposition of tempo and texture there are no other important formal rules that need concern us.

Both overtures in the *Water Music* and *Fireworks Music* follow this basic format, but with typically Handelian modifications. The former features contrasts between two solo violins and the larger group (tutti, or "everyone"), whereas the overture in the *Fireworks Music*, perhaps the largest instrumental piece that Handel ever wrote, includes a quick section that is only nominally contrapuntal. It's really a massive assemblage of vigorous antiphonal fanfares, scales, and heroic motives designed to provide the most vivid burst of energy and excitement possible.

Interestingly, Handel employs a similar melodic motive to lead off each overture, whereas the opening march and ensuing allegro for the *Fireworks Music* also appear, with modified scoring and other adjustments, individually or together in two contemporaneous concertos: the Concerti Grossi HWV 335a and 335b, in D Major and F Major respectively. These pieces are well worth hearing in their own right (the Charles Mackerras recording on Novalis that contains the Largo includes them). It's fascinating to compare the different versions that Handel made, none absolutely identical, of basically the same thematic material. The second movement of HWV 335b also doubles as the finale of 335a, rescored and in a different key; hearing all of this music is sort of like getting acquainted with an entire musical family—parents and children.

Following the overtures, we get the dances and other attractions, some of which are specific to the occasion for which each work was written. Accordingly, in the *Fireworks Music*, which Handel composed to celebrate the Treaty of Aix-la-Chappelle ending the War of the Austrian Succession, we find four movements (or five, depending on how you count them), none of which include the four standard dances previously mentioned. There's a perky Bourrée followed by two character pieces: La Paix ("Peace"), and the work's most famous number, the brassy and percussive La Réjouissance ("Rejoicing"). The suite concludes with a pair of contrasting minuets, one intimate, the next massive—Handel uses the French spelling, Menuet—which bring the work to a grand but graceful conclusion.

The situation with the *Water Music* is more complicated. Handel seems to have intended it as a collection of twenty-two pieces that can be performed in whole or in part, at will. Taken together they run for nearly an hour (as opposed to about twenty minutes for the *Fireworks Music*), but traditionally they have been arranged in three suites characterized by a common key center and scoring. The First Suite (in F) features brilliant writing for horns, instruments which were relatively new in England at the time. The Second Suite (in D) introduces trumpets; the Third (in G) adds flutes (including the high-pitched descant recorder for the folksy final Gigue, sometimes billed as a "Country Dance"). In keeping with the "water" theme, Handel includes two Hornpipes, and the one actually marked "Alla Hornpipe" remains one of the most famous orchestral pieces of the entire baroque period.

Since the manuscript has disappeared and the best contemporary source, which Handel scholar Terence Best discovered only in 2004, sheds no new light on the question, it's up to performers to decide in what order to play the *Water Music*'s various individual pieces, or how to assemble the various suites. For example, most performances place the famous "Trumpet Minuet" at the end of the Third Suite. Handel liked concluding minuets, evidently, but conductor Christopher Hogwood in his recording with the Academy of Ancient Music, noticing that the "Trumpet Minuet" has trumpets, places it with its equally "trumpety" colleagues in the Second Suite. There is no single correct answer, and that only makes listening potentially more interesting.

Remarkably, aside from the Gigue previously mentioned and a single, and singularly lovely Sarabande with flute, none of the other pieces in the *Water Music* include examples of the four standard dances (the allemande and courant), still further testimony to Handel's free-wheeling treatment of period norms. Indeed, the best-known item in the entire work is its third number (in the First Suite), with raucous horns trilling in joyful competition with the strings. The piece has no name, and not even a tempo indication, although it's usually simply called Allegro. It has come to symbolize all that is most "Handelian" in Handel: the catchy bits of melody, rhythmic lift, instrumental brilliance, and the feeling that everyone involved, both players and listeners, is having a jolly good time. The rollicking motive for two horns after the initial fanfare also appears in Melissa'a bravura aria "Desterò dall'empia Dite ogni furia" ("From impious Hell I'll reawaken every fury") from the roughly contemporaneous and quite successful opera *Amadigi* (1715).

Dozens and dozens of excellent versions of both the *Water Music* and *Fireworks Music* are available on both modern and period instruments, some of which even couple the two works together on a single disc. You can find recommendations in the discography at the end of this chapter. However, one recording of the *Fireworks Music*, led by Sir Charles Mackerras with a pickup ensemble (dubbed the "Pro Arte Orchestra") and last available on Testament, deserves special mention. Recorded in 1959, it captures the first modern performance of the piece in Handel's original scoring.

As you can well imagine, getting twenty-four professional oboists together at the same time (the recording actually used a couple extra—twenty-six in all) is just as difficult today as it was in Handel's time—probably more so. The recording sessions used every player available in London and took place from 11:00 p.m. to 2:30 in the morning. Fortified (legend has it) by a great enthusiasm for Handel and plenty of drink, they somehow got through it and turned in a performance of amazing freshness and spontaneity. Fascinatingly, the sound of massed oboes and bassoons, far from being harsh or shrill, actually turns somewhat warm and fuzzy, just as it does with massed strings, no doubt partly a function of the collective vibrato produced by minute pitch variations within each section. This quality is even more evident in the several period instrument versions of the original score that have appeared since. If you love the *Fireworks Music*, this is a "must hear" recording.

Zadok the Priest (1727)

Every time a new monarch or major religious leader gets installed with great ceremony, they have to get smeared with a glob of grease in a process called "anointing." Handel wrote four anthems for the coronation of King George II in 1727, including this one to celebrate the official gunk smearing on the royal brow. It has been performed at the similar stage of every British coronation ceremony since, ten times in all, and on sundry other occasions great and small. Most recently, you can hear *Zadok* in a DirectTV television commercial, where it makes the same impressive physical impact that it always does. Scored for a full orchestra (two oboes, two bassoons, three trumpets, strings [with violins in three parts], timpani and organ continuo)[4] and a seven-part chorus (SSAATBB), *Zadok the Priest* is a knockout. Here is the very short and simple biblical text, taken from 1 Kings:

> A. Zadok the Priest, and Nathan the Prophet anointed Solomon King.
>
> B. And all the people rejoiced, and said:
>
> C. God save the King! Long live the King!
> May the King live for ever,
> Amen, Allelujah.

As you can see, Handel divides the words, which he chose himself, into three sections, which I have marked accordingly. Before the singing starts, however, Handel offers a remarkable prelude, richly scored with violins in three parts. It consists of nothing but rhythm, texture, and harmony, and if you're at all familiar with the "pulse" pieces of the modern minimalist movement (early works by such composers as Philip Glass, Steve Reich, or John Adams), you might be forgiven for believing this to be a particularly iconic example. The effect is calm but massive, an incoming tide or wave of sound that breaks with the entrance of the chorus.

Since the entire anthem lasts only about six minutes, Handel dispatches the text with impressive efficiency. The first section is loudly declamatory, syllabic, and solid. Then, after the anointing of the king, "all the people rejoiced," evidently (the strings suggest) by jumping up and down gleefully. Finally, everyone wishes the king a long reign as joyful polyphony breaks out, with the sense of "may the King live forever" aptly suggested by sustained lines mixing with an "endless" contrapuntal melisma on the word "amen." The effect perfectly captures the celebratory character of the proceedings, but what really makes the piece so remarkable is how cleverly Handel increases the energy and tension from one episode to the next. Clearly, a great dramatist stands behind even this brief occasional work.

As just mentioned, Handel wrote four Coronation Anthems in all, and if you purchase a recording of *Zadok the Priest*, you will mostly likely get (and enjoy) the others. They are:

- *Let Thy Hand Be Strengthened*
- *The King Shall Rejoice*
- *My Heart Is Inditing*

The three remaining pieces are multimovement works, though none is especially long. *My Heart Is Inditing* actually accompanied the coronation of then Queen Caroline, so all four anthems may not be appropriate to every subsequent ceremony. This explains why only *Zadok* has continued to be featured down through the centuries since its premiere. As we all know, the British do pageantry better than anyone, but in 1727 they evidently still needed some practice. The performing forces forgot the anthems' correct order, and according to contemporary testimony generally made a mess of things. Handel for his part, never one to waste good material, subsequently reused much of the music in his later works, *Esther* and *Deborah* especially.

Zadok, with different words, turns up in the revised version of *Esther* along with *My Heart Is Inditing* as originally written. It also makes a terrific closing chorus in *The Occasional Oratorio*. Zadok, the biblical character and not the anthem, shows up quite prominently in the oratorio *Solomon*, where he gets a bunch of attractive arias, including "Sacred raptures cheer my breast" and "Golden columns, fair and bright." In case you were wondering, he's a tenor.

Messiah (1741)

First, a technical note: When I was in high school, some snooty *Messiah* person told me that the correct title of Handel's most iconic work was just that, and not "*The Messiah*." In reality, contemporary sources from Handel's day used both, and when Mozart arranged the oratorio it became, in German, "*Der Messias*," or "*The Messiah*." So, call it whatever you want and don't let anyone tell you otherwise. I now use *Messiah* when referring to the work because saying, "I'm going to see *The Messiah*," sounds a bit too much like I'm running off to join a religious cult whose leader is making megalomaniacal claims for himself. That said, and especially when dealing with music in the eighteenth century, the idea of there being only one unambiguously correct title when most people couldn't even spell their own name the same way twice in succession is laughable.

Messiah's unassailable status in the English-speaking world as the ultimate Christmas piece sometimes results in its being dismissed by those for whom popularity is incompatible with the highest quality. Certainly it is not typical of Handel's oratorios generally. It is one of only two English works with a Christian theme (the other is *Theodora*), and it does not dramatize the life of Jesus Christ in the manner of a typical Passion story. Rather, *Messiah* offers a series of scenes and meditations on the meaning of Christ's sacrifice and the ensuing salvation of mankind. None of the soloists represents a specific character, and nothing ostensibly "happens" in a strictly narrative sense.

That said, while the plot isn't presented dramatically, the music itself is intensely so. To omit discussion of the work entirely, as scholar Winton Dean does in his otherwise classic study *Handel's Dramatic Oratorios*, seems to me to define Handel's art far too narrowly. *Messiah*, whether you call it a sacred oratorio or something else, is as defiantly secular and entertaining as anything else that Handel wrote. I say this not just because some of its most spiritual moments were adapted from earlier, very secular pieces. Melodies from three of Handel's delightful Italian Duets, "No, di vio non vuo fidarme," "Quel fior ch'all'alba ride," and "Se tu non lasci amore,"[5] became six numbers in *Messiah*: "For unto us a Child is born," "All we like sheep have gone astray," "His yoke is easy, His burden is light," "And he shall purify," "O death, where is they sting," and "But thanks be to God."

No, the reason I call the work secular is that this the type of composer Handel was, and he could no more avoid being dramatic and entertaining, even with music on religious themes, than Bach could avoid being spiritual and devotional. This is less a statement about what a piece expresses than a description of how it does so—the mechanism by which it operates. Handel at his most lofty does not often ask that we contemplate or meditate. His universe is almost never static. He wants us to feel the music in our gut, vividly, tactilely, sensually, to the furthest extent that the words permit. This is what accounts for *Messiah*'s popularity to the present day, even among those who are not interested in its religious message.

Handel undoubtedly considered the work's religious message very deeply, but we cannot say that he cared more about *Messiah*'s spirituality than he did about Semele's narcissism, or Bajazet's suicide in the opera *Tamerlano*. *Messiah* holds no monopoly on expressive truth, or depth. Much of Handel's genius as a composer of dramatic music stems from the fact that he could be just as convincing in evoking religious exaltation as he could pagan debauchery. That's why it's silly to make claims about Handel's personal religious sentiments, as the Victorians regularly did, on the basis of *Messiah*'s musical quality. All it proves is that Handel was a great composer who tailored his style to fit innumerable contexts equally well.

After its Dublin premiere in 1741, we know that *Messiah* was played fifty-six times over the remainder of Handel's lifetime. Only a scant number of these performances took place in a sacred context, outside of the theater, and he did not rush to introduce the work in London for fear of offending the religious authorities and the devout among his public. Imagine, a mere "entertainment" about the most sacred possible subject, offered in the theater with a cast that included (gasp!) women. *Messiah* was not, in fact, a success in London initially. It remained a rarity until Handel hit on the idea of using it for benefit concerts to raise money for charity.

One special cause that he supported with particular enthusiasm was London's Foundling Hospital, and it is thanks to the set of parts he donated to that worthy organization that we know for a fact that the continuo group used in early performances consisted of keyboard, four bassoons, three cellos, and two basses, even though the bassoons aren't otherwise mentioned in the score.[6] Handel also wrote an anthem for the Foundling Hospital in 1749, before *Messiah* entered the repertoire, and which ends with none other than the "Hallelujah Chorus." *Messiah* only achieved success, then, incrementally, and it only slowly acquired the "sacred" patina that characterizes our view of it today.

The musical process by which this happened has two components. First, *Messiah* became associated with Christmas, and second, to make it suitable for the season, it was cut to order. Very, very few performances of the work today by community church or choral groups play the piece whole—all two and a half hours of it. What you generally get, even if we ignore the bowdlerized arrangements of the orchestral parts, is a bunch of choruses and a few arias (depending on the availability of soloists) comprising most of part 1 (the Christmas story), some of part 2, and maybe the aria "I know that my Redeemer liveth" from part 3—all concluding with the "Hallelujah Chorus," which technically wraps up the second part as Handel imagined it. And, of course, the performance venue will be a church. Aside from record collectors, not many people actually have heard the true ending that Handel wrote, a glorious choral "Amen" of exquisite beauty and transcendental power.

These typical circumstances of performance effectively crush the drama and tension that Handel's music ought to convey. Choruses, while imposing, tend to be monolithic, particularly when sung by amateurs at ponderously slow tempos. Handel's arias require top-notch operatic soloists, and because the most dramatic are also the most virtuosic, many will be omitted or divested of the necessary ornamentation that gives them extra life. The largest single piece in *Messiah* is the alto aria

"He was despised," a moving lament with a hair-raising quick middle section, "He gave His back to the smiters." It lasts, on average, around nine minutes, and when sung by a first-class soloist in context, at the start of part 2, the effect can be devastating, coming as it does right after the mostly joyous part 1. As usually performed at a Christmas concert, if it's done at all, it can be lethal.

But perhaps the most devastatingly destructive practice in de-dramatizing *Messiah* involves omitting most of the accompanied recitatives, with the usual exception of "Comfort ye, my people" at the very beginning. This requires a bit of explanation. In opera there are two kinds of sung recitation, or "recitative" occurring between the larger numbers (arias, duets, trios, choruses, etc.): secco, or "dry," recitative, which features the voice, keyboard, and (usually) a cello on the bass line, and accompanied recitative (Handel called it simply "accompagnato"), which includes at least the full string section. In baroque music, accompanied recitative is the most dramatic means of expression that there is, being totally freeform and instantaneously illustrative of the text.

Depending on the version performed—as usual, Handel adapted *Messiah* for each new group of performers, so there is no definitive text—the oratorio contains about fifty individual numbers. The recitatives are mostly quite short, there being no intricacies of plot that need explaining in detail. If we take the Bärenreiter Critical Edition as our model, we find seven very brief examples of secco recitative, but nine of accompagnato. This is pretty remarkable when you consider that *Messiah* is supposed to be one of Handel's least dramatic works. Evidently, no one told him that. If the text lacks drama poetically, then fine: he will supply it musically nevertheless.

Some of the most atmospheric and compelling music in *Messiah* occurs in accompanied recitative, numbers such as the bass's "For behold, darkness shall cover the earth," or the large complex of movements for tenor in part 2, beginning with "Thy rebuke hath broken His heart" and concluding with "But Thou didst not leave His soul in hell." This sequence of accompagnato, arioso, accompagnato, and aria really forms a single large structure, and only baroque convention forces Handel to mark it as four separate movements. It demonstrates his concern to create larger blocks of musical continuity, generating an urgent momentum usually lost when *Messiah* gets chopped up and redistributed for the holiday season.

I am not making these points to disparage the tradition of playing *Messiah* at Christmas, or in any other form. As you will see in the discussion of Handel's operas, I encourage listening of every kind, including highlights and aria recitals, especially on recordings into which you can dip at will. We all do it, and not everyone has large chunks of free time available to play complete works at a sitting, or attend long concerts. I do, however, want to draw a distinction between what *Messiah* really is as a work of musical art, and how it is most often used today as an aid to holiday celebrations. At these times, we perceive it more as an object, like a tree or an ornament, and take it for granted; but if you spend the time to get to know it whole, just for itself, you will realize that it really is so much more than that. In other words, give it a shot in August.

Experiencing *Messiah* complete and out of season necessarily involves purchasing a recording. Here are five, listed by conductor, for your consideration:

1. Colin Davis (Philips/Decca): modern instruments, terrific soloists and choir. For many years the reference recording.
2. Charles Mackerras (EMI/Warner): lots of ornamentation in the arias by a Handel specialist and superb conductor generally.
3. Christopher Hogwood (L'Oiseau-Lyre): the performance that legitimized Handel on period instruments.
4. Trevor Pinnock (Achiv): Also on period instruments, grander and in some ways more gripping than Hogwood, and another great solo lineup.
5. Thomas Beecham (RCA): Totally rescored, modern orchestration, with every traditional bad habit imaginable, and an irresistibly compelling reminder of times gone by from a very great conductor playing music he obviously loved.

Chapter I Additional Recommended Recordings

The Harmonious Blacksmith

Paul Nicholson, harpsichord (Hyperion): you get all eight "great" suites. Murray Perahia, piano (Sony Classical): Handel on piano doesn't get any better.

Water Music and *Fireworks Music*

Jordi Savall (Alia Vox): both works on a single disc, wonderfully played on period instruments.

Alexander Gibson (Chandos): Glorious *Water Music* on modern instruments.

Trevor Pinnock (Archiv): he recorded the *Fireworks Music* twice, in both the original (tons of winds) and revised (with strings) scorings.

Zadok the Priest

Robert King (Hyperion): you get the four Coronation Anthems plus the first recording of the *Fireworks Music* in its original scoring on period instruments.

It's Saul *Good*

Exploring the English Oratorios and Associated Instrumental Works

Oratorios and Such, with Recommended Recordings

Il trionfo del Tempo e del Disinganno (1707) [Haim/Erato]
Il trionfo del Tempo e della Verità (1737) [Martini/Naxos]
The Triumph of Time and Truth (1757) [Neville-Towle/
    Delphian]
La Resurrezione (1708) [Minkowski/Archiv]
Aci, Galatea e Polifemo (1708) Serenata [Bonizzoni/Glossa]
Acis and Galatea (1718) Masque [Christie/Erato]
Acis and Galatea (1732) Serenata [no recording]
Esther (1718) [Christophers/Coro]
Esther (1732) [Cummings/Somm]
Brockes Passion (1719) [Neumann/Carus]
Deborah (1733) [King/Hyperion]
Athalia (1733) [Hogwood/L'Oiseau-Lyre]
Parnasso in Festa (1734) Serenata [Hall/Hyperion]
Alexander's Feast (1736) Ode [Gardiner/Decca or
    Christophers/Coro]
Saul (1739) [Jacobs/Harmonia Mundi]
Israel in Egypt (1739) [Parrott/Warner]
Ode for St. Cecilia's Day (1739) [Minkowski/Naive]
L'Allegro, il Penseroso ed il Moderato (1740) Pastoral Ode
    [King/Hyperion]

Messiah (1742) [Pinnock/Archiv]
Samson (1743) [Christophers/Coro]
Semele (1744) Musical Drama [Nelson/Deutsche
    Grammophon]
Joseph and His Brethren (1744) [King/Hyperion]
Hercules (1745) Musical Drama [Minkowski/Archiv]
Belshazzar (1745) [Pinnock/Archiv]
The Occasional Oratorio (1746) [King/Hyperion]
Judas Maccabaeus (1747) [McGegan/Harmonia Mundi]
Joshua (1748) [King/Hyperion]
Alexander Balus (1748) [King/Hyperion]
Susanna (1749) [McGegan/Harmonia Mundi]
Solomon (1749) [Reuss/Harmonia Mundi]
Theodora (1750) [Christie/Erato]
The Choice of Hercules (1751) [King/Hyperion]
Jephtha (1752) [Gardiner/Decca]

Instrumental Works, with Recommended Recordings

Overtures [Pinnock/Archiv]
Concerti Grossi Opp. 3 and 6 [Egarr (Op. 3) & Manze (Op.
    6) both Harmonia Mundi]
Complete Organ Concertos Opp. 4 and 7, + three more
    [Pinnock/Archiv]
Concerto in *Alexander's Feast* [See Gardiner for complete
    work, above]
Concerti a Due Cori [Mackerras/Novalis]

It's difficult to look at this chapter's list of works without feeling a bit of panic. It includes all of Handel's largest, full-scale, theoretically nonoperatic vocal output, plus all the orchestral pieces that he may have derived from them or composed to go along with them in performance. It's just a staggering amount of music, and a terrifying testament to Handel's industriousness, especially when you consider that he was not just the composer, but also the conductor, keyboard soloist, impresario, ticket vendor—you name it. Nevertheless, in this chapter I propose to seize the bull by the horns and cover each work, or group of works, in sufficient detail so that if you find your curiosity piqued, you will come to the experience of listening armed with at least one useful fact or dedicated object of your attention.

Initially, however, let us try to answer a threshold question: What is an oratorio? In Handel's day there were many terms in addition to *oratorio* for extended vocal works that were not operas. A shorter piece was generally thought of as a *cantata*, whereas anything else could be an *ode*, a *masque*, or a *serenata*, among other terms. After Handel invented the "English oratorio," the answer became: "An oratorio is an extended work for orchestra, soloists, and choir on a biblical or sacred subject, given in concert form."

However, I prefer the looser, practical definition current in Handel's own time, since this corresponds more accurately to what he actually wrote: "An oratorio may be any extended vocal work that is not an opera and therefore is not staged." This does not mean that an oratorio *cannot* be staged; some of Handel's have been, and you could even argue that they deserve to be, but the point is that, at least originally, they were not. Also, there have always been large, dramatic choral works that defy categorization. In the nineteenth century, Berlioz's *The Damnation of Faust* and Saint-Saëns's *Samson and Delilah* are just two of the best known. Both can be staged as operas or sung in concert, as oratorios. The Saint-Saëns, although usually performed as an opera, fits the conventional definition of oratorio particularly well, being an extended vocal work with extensive choral participation based on a biblical subject. Of course, Handel wrote a *Samson* too.

The more rigid, post-Handelian definition of *oratorio* arose, first of all, to create a unique category of English music with Handel as its founder and figurehead. Second, it flattered the endless parade of second-rate composers who came later with the notion that they were writing "sacred" (and therefore "serious," or at all events "worthy") works just because they may have taken their subject matter from the

Bible or some other religious source. I would argue, to the contrary, that this is the precise reason that nineteenth-century English music constitutes such a long, dull litany of failure in vocal productions from start to finish (Arthur Sullivan always excepted), and that Handel succeeded because he never worked under the illusion that he was writing sacred music, notwithstanding the source of his texts. In other words, he understood the difference between entertainment written on a sacred subject, and actual sacred music designed to facilitate worship.

Some of the librettos that Handel set are more overtly "religious" than others, and in some the drama sits rather uneasily next to the need to moralize about monotheism versus paganism, and whatnot. The poster child for this sort of tension is probably *Alexander Balus*, a story of war, love, and treachery that has absolutely nothing to do with religion or anything especially sacred; and where, at the end, after everyone is either dead or exiled, the Maccabean leader Jonathan can do nothing but say, "Well, if everyone had believed in the one true God none of this would have happened." The concluding obligatory chorus of praise, cast in a glum minor key, tells us that neither the Jews nor Handel are having any of it.

The same observation applies to Handel's final wholly new oratorio, *Jephtha*, the story of a noble military leader who agrees to sacrifice the first person he sees on returning from battle if God grants him victory. This is, in fact, a devil's bargain because that person naturally happens to be his innocent, beloved daughter, but the story has nothing to do with the truths of the Judeo-Christian tradition. It's a legend as old as civilization itself, and many cultures have some version of it. Mozart's *Idomeneo* presents exactly the same situation (only a son, not a daughter), with characters out of Greek mythology. Neither God, nor the gods in the latter case, ultimately accepts the foolishly offered sacrifice. The one concession to Judeo-Christian morality is that Jephtha's daughter, Iphis, gets to spend the rest of her life serving God as a virgin—a distasteful concession to contemporary taste easily addressed with a few strategic cuts toward the end.

What matters, basically, is that in all of these situations where drama and the assertion of specific religious doctrine come into conflict, drama wins. If Handel sometimes writes religious-sounding music in his oratorios, it is because some of his characters (including that collective character, the chorus) express religious sentiments. They are appropriate to the context. Honest observer of human nature that he is, Handel takes these feelings as seriously as any other emotion that the events being depicted require him to evoke; but he does not sit in sanctimonious judgment at the cost of realistic characterization.

Indeed, Handel places all of his characters, even the evil ones, on a surprisingly equal musical footing. Bloodthirsty Queen Athalia in the eponymous oratorio, a singularly rich musical portrait, often gets cited as a case in point. Commentators also have often mentioned that Handel's heathens, in such works as *Athalia, Deborah, Samson, Alexander Balus, Belshazzar,* or *Theodora,* get to "live it up" with some of his most enjoyable music, whereas the Israelites, theoretically the good guys, do a lot of kvetching and moaning until the inevitable victory over their foes gets Handel going in his inimitable "Hallelujah" mode. Actually, in *Theodora* it's the Christians who do the kvetching and moaning, but the point is that Handel's refusal to treat his subjects musically as simplistic essays in black and white gives his works vividness, realism, and much of their emotional power, even if the ending remains a foregone conclusion.

Another reason to adopt a more liberal definition of the term "oratorio" is that, if we consider the above list of works, it becomes clear that Handel wrote oratorios, or works of similar character, throughout his career. He did not stop writing operas and start writing oratorios from scratch, at the flick of a switch, after 1741, the date of his last operatic premier. The fifteen years of London's Royal Academy (1719–34), of which he was general manager, was the only period in which Handel was basically wholly dedicated to operatic composition and production. This picture, then, offers us a more nuanced view of his artistic development, and suggests that his focus on oratorio in the last decades of his life emerged gradually, but naturally, over time.

Even if we were to limit ourselves to works traditionally called oratorios, or usually classed with them, the differences in substance and approach from one work to the next remain astonishing and unpredictable. Handel's two early Italian oratorios, *Il trionfo del Tempo e del Disinganno* and *La Resurrezione,* are operas in form but not in subject matter: they lack a dramatic story line. The English works, on the other hand, for the most part are operatic in subject matter, but oratorios on account of the prominent role given to the chorus, but even that isn't dispositive. Both *Semele* and *Hercules* are classed as "musical drama," which is code for "opera," and that really is what they are. Both have been successfully staged in recent decades. Handel referred to the English masque *Acis and Galatea* as an opera at one point (in addition to calling it just about everything else). He liked to call his settings of biblical stories "sacred dramas." The later odes and serenatas are essentially oratorios conceptually similar to the early Italian pieces, even if the level of choral participation is greater.

Aside from the two Roman oratorios, which fall into two big halves, Handel's full-scale English works in the form are similar in structure to his operas. Most contain three parts, or acts, totaling roughly fifty numbers parceled out among arias, secco and accompanied recitative, ensembles (duets, trios, choruses, etc.), orchestral interludes, and an overture, often in several movements. The total playing time ranges on average from two and a half to three and a half hours, not including any concertos or other diversions that Handel might have included at his concerts. English audiences paid attention to overall length and balked at any work felt to be too short to justify the cost of a ticket.

Let's turn to the music. I think that a topical approach offers the most effective strategy for covering the remaining individual works, so I have reorganized the big list at the start of this chapter into seven mini-essays covering a range of subjects, bearing in mind that often a specific piece fits into more than one category. You'll find this helpful. These are big, rich, multifaceted pieces, then, and the more they defy easy characterization, the more opportunities for listener appeal they present.

Blood and Guts

The second act of Handel's *Solomon* largely concerns the famous "cut the baby in half" judgment, resolving the dispute between two feuding harlots as to which is the child's real mother. Friedrich Chrysander, who edited the first (and still only) mostly complete Handel edition in the second half of the nineteenth century, shared the Victorian decorousness of the period and labeled the two women "maidens," which they most certainly were not. They were harlots, and that's what Handel and his audiences called them. It was, in many ways, a more honest age. Even today, you're not likely to find a biographical squib in a program booklet for a notable singer that reads, "Madame X created a sensation at the Royal Albert Hall with her gripping portrayal of the Second Harlot in Handel's *Solomon*." It's just not done.

We all know that the Bible, the Old Testament in particular, describes plenty of violence and brutality, but Handel's oratorio librettos, far from minimizing it, embrace it with gusto. Graphic sexual imagery may have been taboo, but gratuitous violence? No problem. The result, when paired with Handel's powerful music, gives even the most stilted language an impact that is visceral and perhaps even shocking. Later in this same scene in *Solomon*, after Harlot Number Two has approved the royal decree to divide the baby equally between the two women, Harlot Number One sings the following mournful aria:

> Can I see my infant gor'd
> With the fierce relentless sword?
> Can I see him yield his breath,
> Smiling at the hand of death?
> And behold the purple tides
> Gushing down his tender sides?
> Rather be my hopes beguil'd,
> Take him all, but spare my child.

The imagery verges on the expressionist, but it gives this heavily stylized situation an emotional edge, a grit even, that's very real, and impossible to deny.

Scenes like this one, characterized by similar language, permeate the biblical oratorios. Here is another example, this time from *Samson*, right after the description of his destruction of the Philistine temple. It's only a recitative, but it's just the thing to put you in the mood for the famous "Dead March"—the same one used previously in *Saul*, by the way—that immediately follows.

Proceed we hence to find his body
Soak'd in vile Philistine blood; with the pure stream,
And cleansing herbs wash off his clodded gore;
Then solemnly attend him to my tomb
With silent obsequies, and fun'ral train.

And speaking of "clodded gore," how about this gem from the very first scene for the Baal-worshipping, Israelite-hating title character of one of Handel's greatest but least known oratorios, *Athalia*?

She, pale, from my embrace withdrew,
And bleeding limbs lay mangled in my view;
The horrid carnage dogs contending tore,
And drank with dreadful thirst the floating gore.

Perhaps the most shocking moment in all of the Handel oratorios occurs in the third act of *Deborah*, when the Israelite woman Jael describes with bloodthirsty relish how she dispatched the Canaanite captain Sissera by nailing his head to the floor of her tent:

When from the battle that proud captain fled,
Vengeance divine to my pavilion led
The trembling fugitive; who, pale with care,
Besought me, panting, to conceal him there;
With flaming thirst, and anguish in his look,
He ask'd for water from the limpid brook;
But milk I gave him in a copious bowl;
With ecstacy he quaff'd, and cooled his soul,
And then, with his laborious flight opprest,
In some few moments he sunk down to rest.
Then I was conscious, Heav'n, that happy hour
Had placed the foe of Judah in my pow'r:
The workman's hammer and a nail I seized,
And whilst his limbs in deep repose he eas'd,
I through his bursting temples forc'd the wound,
And rivetted the tyrant to the ground.

This climactic scene, followed by Jael's celebratory aria "Tyrant, now no more we dread thee," largely accounts for the fact that *Deborah* has never quite caught on with modern audiences expecting "nice" sacred music. Handel's public had no such scruples and enjoyed it thoroughly, so there is no reason why anyone who likes, say, Quentin Tarantino movies, shouldn't as well.

The situation of the eponymous heroine in *Theodora* is just as harrowing and even more personal, although the language is a tad more discreet (it involves sex, after all). Her Roman captor Valens, after sentencing her to servitude as a prostitute for her Christian faith, offers this ultimatum:

> Return, Septimius, to the stubborn maid,
> And learn her final resolution.
> If ere the sun with prone career has reach'd
> The western isles, she deigns an offering
> To the great gods, who subjected the world
> To conqu'ring Rome, she shall be free; if not,
> The meanest of my guards with lustful joy
> Shall triumph o'er her boasted chastity.

After this horrific decree, the depraved heathens celebrate Theodora's impending rape in this frothy, horn-led chorus:

> Venus laughing from the skies,
> Will applaud her votaries.
> While seizing the treasure
> We revel in pleasure,
> Revenge sweet love supplies.

Even *Susanna*, which is technically a pastoral comedy, at least for much of the time, launches its third act with a pitilessly gleeful chorus of Babylonians singing the following perky rhyming couplet:

> The cause is decided, the sentence decreed,
> Susanna is guilty, Susanna must bleed.

Naturally, there is nothing new in death penalties, bloody vendettas, mass murder, or scenes of sadistic cruelty in the context of entertainment, especially where (as here) the good guys win and the bad guys pay. Today, however, we universally condemn the idea of religion as justification for such atrocities whenever they happen. Only fanatics and terrorists still make the case for them. Additionally, our modern view of *Messiah* as the archetypal Handel masterpiece has warped our perspective on what a biblical oratorio really describes.

If the sentiments expressed in these examples clearly don't belong in a place of worship, just keep in mind that Handel intended these pieces for the theater, *Messiah* included. Granted that the emphasis there remains mostly on the message of spiritual salvation, but Handel and his librettist, Charles Jennens, still could not resist sticking some disturbing imagery from the Book of Isaiah into the "B" section of the great lament, "He was despised." Let us not forget, "He gave His back to the smiters, and His cheeks to them that plucked off the hair. He hid not His face from shame and spitting."

Extreme situations such as these are the lifeblood of the theater, and those in the Bible are as graphic, and therefore as suitable for dramatic treatment, as any. In setting these subjects, Handel didn't have to moderate or restrain his natural theatrical impulses at all. On the contrary: the biblical origins of these stories provided cover for scenes of violence that would have been impossible to present visually on the operatic stage of the day, where most of the nastiness took place out of sight and had to be described at second hand anyway. To this extent the lack of restrictions imposed by the conventions of *opera seria*, as we shall see, arguably set him free.

The Waratorios

The Occasional Oratorio (1746)
Judas Maccabaeus (1747)
Joshua (1748)
Alexander Balus (1748)

On leaving Italy and before settling in England, in 1710, Handel took a job in Hanover, Germany, at the house of the elector, Prince George, who in 1714 became King George I of England. By then, Handel had already been in London for several years, having decided to remain permanently in 1712 (with or without his employer's permission).

Notwithstanding this potential snafu, Handel got along well with the royal family. He taught their children, received a lifetime stipend from the treasury, and wrote music for important occasions. It has even been suggested that one of the reasons for his first journey to England may have been to feel out the territory and gather some precoronation intelligence.

During much of the eighteenth century, Europe was at war for one reason or another. It was very much a normal state of affairs, and it is only to be expected that this would be reflected in Handel's music. The biblical oratorios, in particular, often describe a state of war either as the background to the story (consider *Belshazzar* and *Samson*) or as its principal subject. Handel's audiences, as we have seen, accepted the Bible at face value, including the concept of righteous slaughter and violence perpetrated in the name of the Lord. Recall these lines in "Welcome, welcome mighty King!" from *Saul*:

> Saul, who hast thy thousands slain,
> Welcome to thy friends again!
> David his ten thousands slew,
> Ten thousand praises are his due!

Israel in Egypt, the otherwise uplifting story of the liberation of the Israelites from bondage in Egypt, also includes plenty of smiting and slaying even apart from the graphic portrayal of the Ten Plagues. Handel famously celebrates the destruction of the Egyptian army with the doctrinally alarming duet "The Lord is a man of war," for two basses:

> The Lord is a man of war: Lord is His name.
> Pharaoh's chariots and his host hath He cast into the sea;
> his chosen captains also are drowned in the Red Sea.

During Handel's residence in England, he lived through multiple local and European conflicts, most of which had a religious component (Catholics versus Protestants), with quite a few requiring him to write appropriately commemorative music. Biographers tend to sniff at these works as bombastic puffery unworthy of his genius, but we have no evidence that Handel's patriotic sentiments were not sincere, or his loyalty to the Crown anything but genuine. If you take a look at the list of wars fought during Handel's lifetime, you can see that his musical involvement was substantial:

- War of the Spanish Succession (1701–13) [Utrecht Te Deum and Jubilate]
- Jacobite Uprising of 1715
- Anglo-Spanish War (1727–29)
- War of the Austrian Succession (1740–48) [Dettingen Te Deum and Dettingen Anthem; *Royal Fireworks Music*]
- Jacobite Uprising of 1745 [The Four "Waratorios"]
- Seven Years' War (1756–63)

The period 1746–48 was particularly productive in this respect. During 1745, the year of the Jacobite rebellion, prodded by the French, the (Catholic) Stuart family led by "Bonnie Prince Charlie" gathered a force in Scotland to try to claim the throne from the (Protestant) house of Hanover, then held by George II. As far as uprisings go, this one was well timed, since most of the English army was in Europe fighting the War of the Austrian Succession, and it almost succeeded—or so it seemed to a nervous London populace. The rebellion was definitively put down at the Battle of Culloden in April 1746. In such tense times, a series of patriotic, chest-pounding oratorios seemed just the ticket, and Handel responded with gusto.

Of the four "Waratorios" (as I like to call them), only one, *Judas Maccabaeus*, proved a lasting success. *Joshua* still gets trotted out now and then, but the other two might as well never have existed. They join *Joseph and His Brethren* at the bottom of the Handel oratorio popularity sweepstakes among both general and specialist audiences. As regards *Joseph*, the critics have a point, and not because the poetry is bad on a number-by-number basis. Even the oft-ridiculed aria "Ah jealousy, thou pelican" makes sense if you know anything about the mythology of pelicans (Google it and see for yourself). The problems with *Joseph* are macroscopic. The story as presented offers Handel no opportunity at all for interesting characterization born of conflict, or for powerful extended situations of confrontation between the protagonists.

As we saw in the discussion about *Messiah*, Handel was perfectly capable of creating a gripping dramatic entity out of a text with no plot at all in the conventional sense. *Joseph*, however, thanks to librettist James Miller (who Handel never used again), promises a good story and then delivers nothing but a series of disconnected scenes that make it impossible for the composer to create any sustained momentum or movement to a climax. This is a crime. The Handel literature, and critical writing on music generally, is full of condemnation of works that fail to live up to standards and strictures that they never attempt to fulfill in the first place, but in looking askance at *Joseph* the critics have a point. The music may be fine as it stands; it just doesn't add up to anything special.

I offer this digression on *Joseph* here so that we don't have to discuss the piece further, and also because this comparative failure makes an excellent contrast to the four Waratorios. The first of them, *The Occasional Oratorio*, is a colorful celebration of patriotism and loyalty similar in concept, if not in message, to *Messiah*. Much of it is thrilling. As noted previously, it ends with a version of *Zadok the Priest*, and finales don't get grander than that. Before we get there, however, Handel provides a splendid overture in four movements—practically a concerto by itself—followed by great extended pieces, such as the aria and chorus, "Be wise, be wise at length"; the deeply moving aria "O liberty, thou choicest treasure"; and several adaptations of the best choruses from *Israel in Egypt*. Handel scholars often suggest that the composition of *The Occasional Oratorio* was a rushed job; but if so, there's not much sign of it in the finished product.

The other three works have powerful stories to tell, and that's exactly what they do in their various ways. Handel's librettist for these, Thomas Morrell, has also come in for his load of guff, and no one would claim that this aria from *Judas Maccabaeus* is masterly poetry:

> Pious orgies, pious airs,
> Decent sorrow, decent pray'rs,
> Will to the Lord ascend, and move
> His pity, and regain His love.

But with all due respect to the self-styled literary critics (and virtually all musical scholars writing about vocal music fancy themselves literary critics, especially if they are British), none of that matters if the librettist gets the basics of the plot down coherently. Morrell does that, and Handel "handles" the rest.

One of the reasons we tend not to hear the other Waratorios regularly is because Handel took some of their best numbers and stuffed them into his revised version of *Judas Maccabaeus*. "O liberty, thou choicest treasure," just mentioned, eventually wound up in *Judas*, as did its most famous single number, "See, the conqu'ring hero comes!" which Handel originally wrote for *Joshua* (it's still there, too). However, these latter two works have a lot more in common than just a popular chorus.

Both take as their main character not their titular heroes, but the Jewish people, as represented by the chorus. In *Judas* this strategy gets emphasized by the fact that, aside from Judas and his brother Simon (and later the Jewish ambassador to Rome), the bulk of the solo singing goes to an unnamed couple simply called "Israelitish Man" and "Israelitish Woman." These two characters act as more intimate extensions of the chorus, adding contrast without compromising its collective identity. As we have already mentioned (and sampled), the work ends with one of Handel's most effective pieces in "Hallelujah" mode.

Joshua has a bit more variety, including a love story as a subplot, but the concept is pretty much the same. While the winsome Achsah gets two lovely, lyrical arias that have since become popular as recital numbers ("Hark! 'tis the linnet and the thrush" and "Oh! Had I Jubal's lyre"), it's the big choral frescoes in act 2, including the destruction of Jericho and Joshua's command that the sun stand still in the sky, that make the piece so much fun to listen to. In both of these oratorios, the action is swift and the contrasts bold. The chorus moves back and forth, somewhat schizophrenically we must admit, from the depths of depression to the heights of exaltation, goaded on by the rallying cries of its warrior hero.

The tale of *Alexander Balus* is considerably more operatic, and the work contains at least once character sketch of considerable depth and sensitivity: that of Cleopatra, who gets a chapter in this book to herself later on. There's also a contrasting chorus of "Asiates" to spice up the ensemble writing; but then, Handel scores all four of the Waratorios with a particularly lavish hand, offering plenty of vivid instrumental color amid the trumpets and drums of battle and rejoicing. Subtle these works are not. On the other hand, taking an analogy from Hollywood, action movies aren't supposed to be as sophisticated and thought provoking as art films. Both have their merits, and nothing prevents enthusiasts from enjoying each for what it is.

Pastoral Fantasies

Il trionfo del Tempo e del Disinganno (1707)
Il trionfo del Tempo e della Verità (1737)
The Triumph of Time and Truth (1757)
Aci, Galatea e Polifemo (1708) Serenata
Acis and Galatea (1718) Masque or Pastoral Opera
Acis and Galatea, (1732) Serenata
Parnasso in Festa (1734) Serenata
Alexander's Feast (1736) Ode
Ode for St. Cecilia's Day (1739)
L'Allegro, il Penseroso ed il Moderato (1740)
Susanna, (1749)
The Choice of Hercules (1751)

You might call the works listed here "the lovable Handel," because his music in pastoral mode not only represents him at his most inimitable from a stylistic point of view, but much of it was designed to captivate the ear in an especially vivid and direct way. It really plays to his strengths as a composer. For example, if you're looking for the perfect introduction to Handel's sound world and don't have a lot of free time on hand, try the *Ode for St. Cecilia's Day*. It's music composed in celebration of music—so is *Alexander's Feast*, by the way—and it does everything a Handel choral work is supposed to do, but it only requires about an hour.

You get an overture that became most of the Concerto Grosso Op. 6, No. 5, a stirring march, and a series of splendid descriptive arias featuring, respectively, solo cello, a martial trumpet, a delightfully warbling flute (and equally warbling soprano—in the recommended recording the spectacular Lucy Crowe), the massed violins, and finally the organ. Then there are the choruses, including a final contrapuntal tour de force on the text "The dead shall live, the living die, and Music shall untune the sky." God only knows what that last phrase means. I guess it doesn't matter as long as it rhymes. In any case, the result is glorious and distinctly more lyrical than Handel in his usual "Hallelujah" mode.

The pastoral was a major topic in baroque music and poetry, indeed, in Western art generally. In its simplest iteration, it encompasses music about, or evocative, of nature, but of course *nature* can be defined in many ways. There is the "natural" association of specific instruments with various iconic ideas and images: flutes with birdsong, oboes with shepherd's pipes and therefore the outdoors more generally, trumpets with battle, horns with the hunt, strings with ocean waves, winds, and (violins) with birds again. All of these conventions Handel recognized and frequently employed.

Music itself was thus a reflection of the natural world, and so such works as the *Ode for St. Cecilia's Day* and *Alexander's Feast*, both composed in honor of the patron saint of music, properly belong to the pastoral tradition. The full title of the latter is *Alexander's Feast, or The Power of Music: An Ode, in Honor of St. Cecilia's Day*, and the text, for the most part, is by seventeenth-century poet John Dryden (who also wrote the other ode that Handel set a few years later). Here, however, instead of a list of characteristics of various music instruments, we get a real story.

Alexander (the Great) and his courtesan Thaïs (no relation to the heroine of the eponymous Massenet opera) are holding a big celebration in the city of Persepolis in honor of the conquest of Persia. Egged on by Thaïs, the old minstrel Timotheus exploits the power of music to induce various passions in Alexander. He gets him drunk with a rousing song in praise of Bacchus (with sensational horn writing), and when intoxication threatens to turn violent makes him mournful with a lament for dead King Darius. Next music arouses Alexander to the pleasures of love, and for the grand finale, "Revenge, Timotheus cries" against the Persians for Greek lives lost. Thaïs then calls for a bit of digestive smiting, leading the revelers out of the hall with torches lit to burn down the conquered city, gleefully killing as many Persians as possible in the process.

It should be clear from all of this, so far at least, that the power of music on pagans is not entirely beneficial. One thing, however, is certain: as always with Handel, his pagans really know how to party. Such lines as "The Many rend the skies with loud Applause; So Love was crown'd, but Musick won the Cause" practically beg Handel (and his chorus) to pull no punches, Dryden's moralizing notwithstanding. As a coda, Alexander and his crew vanish into the mists of time, and at last St. Cecilia appears, demonstrating the spiritual virtue of music by playing the organ—for which purpose Handel had handy his own Organ Concerto in G Minor, Op. 4 No. 1—and all ends as it should, with an evening "Sacred to Harmony and Love." Significantly the words of this last chorus are by Handel's collaborator Newburgh Hamilton, suggesting that Handel might have had his own ideas about "the power of Musick." However, it is also common to omit this final bit and end the work with the preceding chorus, "Let old Timotheus yield the prize," staying closer to Dryden's original.

St. Cecilia, incidentally, allegedly was a Roman noblewoman and virgin (naturally) who was martyred in a manner worthy of Rasputin. First the emperor (Alexander Severus or possibly Marcus Aurelius) attempted to lock her in her sauna in the hopes of making her sweat to death. When that didn't work, she was beheaded—three times, officially—but still survived for another three days before succumbing to her wounds. She became the patron saint of music because she "sang to God in her heart" at her (arranged) wedding ceremony, having previously vowed to remain a virgin, and told her husband that he would suffer divine punishment if he consummated their marriage. He had his doubts. So she proved it by showing up, guardian angel in tow and symbolically decked in flowers, at his conversion to Christianity. She's been the patron saint of music ever since.

Alexander's Feast proved to be so popular that Handel's publisher, John Walsh, issued it by subscription in full score. Still, its composer had a problem. As written, the work lasts about an hour and a half, not long enough for a full evening's entertainment. Handel addressed this is numerous ways over the years. At the first performances in 1736 he added the organ concerto just mentioned, plus the Harp Concerto Op. 4, No. 6 (published as an organ concerto in the context of Op. 4) describing how Timotheus "with flying Fingers touch'd the Lyre," and also the Concerto Grosso in C Major, HWV318, as an interlude. He even tossed in an Italian cantata for soprano and tenor, *Cecilia, volgi un sguardo*, HWV89, for good measure.

Of the recommended recordings, Harry Christophers on Coro, my preferred version, offers the two Op. 4 concertos in their appropriate spots. John Eliot Gardiner, on Decca, gives you the Concerto in C Major, which has become known for obvious reasons as the "Alexander's Feast" Concerto. Gardiner also picks up some of Handel's later revisions to the score, but Christophers offers the most complete and musically satisfying *Alexander's Feast* experience. The scoring, by the way, is Handel at his richest: recorders, oboes, bassoons, horns, trumpets, timpani, plus a varied continuo section (organ, harpsichord, theorbo), with the usual imaginatively varied string textures. If you want the Italian cantata, too, Robert King has recorded it for Hyperion as the coupling to his excellent version of the *Ode for St. Cecilia's Day*.

Another angle on the pastoral topic that we often find in Handel is what we might call the "dramatic pastoral": stories involving shepherds, nymphs, and other mythological characters, all set in the Arcadian countryside of ancient Greece. Handel acquired a foundation for this sort of writing in Italy, where he wrote around a hundred cantatas and other pieces, many of which set poetry involving typical pastoral characters and their well-known stories. He was fantastically good at this sort of thing, as it turned out, and the habits he learned stayed with him for his entire career. The "pastoral opera" *Acis and Galatea* (as well as the earlier Italian serenata on the same story), the opera *Atalanta*, and the glorious royal wedding serenata *Parnasso in Festa*, all belong to this tradition. We will take a closer look at the two settings of the *Acis* story in the next chapter.

The central act of *Parnasso*, incidentally, treats the myth of Orpheus and Eurydice, and also explores the theme of the power of music, much as *Alexander's Feast* would do a few years later. Although much of *Parnasso* resets music originally composed for *Athalia*, which had not yet been heard in London, there is also substantial new material. All of it is of top quality, and often the use to which the preexisting numbers get put is very different from their initial context. For example, the chorus "The gods who chosen blessings shed," a throwaway number in *Athalia* that sets the scene for the first appearance of the queen herself, makes an absolutely superb conclusion to the second act of *Parnasso* as "Coralli e perle vogliamo offrir" ("Let us offer coral and pearls"). The music, in its rhythm, melody, and ebullient scoring for horns, sounds remarkably like a close relative of the first movement of Beethoven's Seventh Symphony. All in all, *Parnasso* is a gem, one that has been almost totally and unfairly disregarded by posterity. Fortunately its single recording (on Hyperion) is magnificent.

Even a comparative failure with the public, such as the opera *Il pastor fido* ("The Faithful Shepherd") had a special place in Handel's heart, judging from his ongoing revisions and revivals. He clearly placed great confidence in his "pastoral" works and wanted the public to share his enthusiasm, especially since music evoking an Arcadian setting proved readily adaptable to similar stories from other sources: take, for example, the biblical tale of "Susanna and the Elders." The result is Handel's single biblical oratorio containing plausible comic characters. Here, the lecherous elders fulfill the role of the foolish, amorous nymphs of classical mythology.

Finally the natural world, as understood in Handel's time at least, included *human* nature, and the larger spiritual dimension represented by God as the creator and master of all. We already see this conception underpinning the two pieces dedicated to St. Cecilia. Three of the works in the list at the start of this section belong in this category of "pastoral allegory," or morality play: the *Triumph of Time and Truth* in all three of its incarnations, *L'Allegro, il Penseroso ed il Moderato*, and *The Choice of Hercules*. They deserve a closer look, as the first two especially are key pieces in Handel's output, if for different reasons.

The character of Hercules figures prominently in three of Handel's works. First, there was the opera *Admeto* (1727), whose story is better known when it takes the name of his wife, Alceste, as in Gluck's famous opera. You may know the story from Greek mythology: Alceste agrees to die in place of her sick husband, and Hercules has to go down to Hades to bring her back. Next came the "musical drama" in English,

Hercules (1745), which is discussed later. Finally, in 1750, Handel assembled a little one-act oratorio on the young Hercules's need to decide between Pleasure and Virtue. Needless to say, he picks virtue with the paradoxical twist that, as in all such cases, we have a whopping good time listening to him make his decision. It's not as if Handel asks him, or us, to swallow a dose of musical medicine because it's healthy rather than enjoyable.

The Choice of Hercules has an interesting origin. Much of the piece began life as incidental music for a play: *Alceste*. That production was canceled, leaving Handel with about fifty minutes of music that he clearly cared about. The original *Alceste* score has been recorded a couple of times, most notably by Christopher Hogwood for the L'Oiseau-Lyre label, and more recently by Christian Cumyn on Chandos, so you can sample it if you like. In any event, working with his usual breathtaking speed, Handel took about a week to refashion the piece as an "interlude" on the Hercules myth, which he performed as additional entertainment at performances of the always-too-short *Alexander's Feast* (either at the end as an additional act, or in the middle between the two parts). The story of Alceste, as already mentioned, contains a substantial role for Hercules as well, so there's a certain logic in Handel's strategy here.

There is a very long history of using a classical subject, and this one in particular, to illustrate what is basically a Christian allegory in favor of virtuous living. Bach set the same tale in his secular cantata *Hercules auf dem Scheideweg* ("Hercules at the Crossroads"), much of which found a final home in his *Christmas Oratorio*. Handel's scoring is typically rich: the pastoral character highlighted through the generous use of flutes, oboes, bassoon, and horns. Virtue's first big aria, "This manly youth's exalted mind," with twittering solo flute and violin, is scarcely less sexy than Pleasure's preceding music, while the Attendant on Pleasure's sole number, "Enjoy the sweet Elysian grove," paints the seductive woodland scene.

Handel makes no effort to conceal the delightful paradox at work in making Virtue's music even more pleasurable than Pleasure—evidence of his clear understanding that, whatever the outcome, it can only be achieved by sensual means. The voice parts, consistent with the theme of seduction of one kind or another, are all high: Pleasure is a soprano;

Virtue, a mezzo soprano or alto; Hercules himself is an alto castrato (a typical convention of the period for young men); and only the "bit part" of An Attendant on Pleasure is a tenor. The chorus supplies additional weight and contrast, assisted by a pair of trumpets.

The Choice of Hercules is another one of those pieces that often gets overlooked in discussions of Handel's output, but like the *Ode for St. Cecilia's Day*, it does just about everything his larger works do, only in less than an hour. It has been very well recorded, with the Hyperion version recommended at the head of this chapter particularly outstanding. Give it some thought if you want a Handel fix but you're on a tight schedule.

Handel's pastoral ode *L'Allegro, il Penseroso ed il Moderato* translates as "The Cheerful Man, the Thoughtful [or Serious] Man, and the Temperate Man." It has always been seen as one of his most original and masterful creations. I love the piece, and you will too. Playing for almost exactly two hours, it is also one of Handel's more compact large works. It has no "filler." As in *Messiah*, the lack of action has forced Handel to produce a sort of inner dramatic momentum by purely musical means. There are very few secco recitatives: most are fully accompanied with the result that individual numbers tend to cluster into larger blocks of continuous music. The result, unusually full of variety and contrast even for Handel, is uniquely satisfying.

I do, however, take issue with the way the piece usually gets described. Most of the text of the first two parts consists of an interweaving of two early poems ("L'Allegro" and "Il Penseroso") by John Milton. Now, as we all know, Milton is a great poet, although, having suffered through an entire semester of *Paradise Lost* and other examples of his output, I often find his poetry dull. There's too much "penseroso" and not enough "allegro" for my taste. Besides, modern listeners are likely to find *all* of Handel's texts—even the biblical ones—archaic, mangled in syntax, oblique in meaning, and full of confounding allusion. It comes with the territory. Most commentators give Milton much of the credit—too much in my view—for the success of the work, resorting lazily to some version of the old cliché "great poetry inspires great music."

This view assumes that Handel knew great English poetry when he saw it, that he cared about this aspect particularly when selecting his texts, that he agreed with the common assessment that it was great in the first place, that he took pains to preserve its literary integrity in his musical settings, and that the very qualities that make it great are somehow enshrined in tones. It utterly ignores the fact that many of Handel's (and everyone else's, for that matter) most inspired works are settings of mediocre, even terrible poetry, and it asks listeners to hold certain musical works in higher regard based on literary rather than musical criteria. In other words, this perspective fundamentally misstates the relationship between the composer and the words he set, as well as his reasons for doing so.

If great poetry really mattered so much to Handel, 95 percent of his works never would have been composed in the first place. That's a fact. What Handel wanted wasn't "great" poetry in a literary sense, but *effective* poetry—words that provided the best possible excuse for writing music. In this regard, more credit should go to his collaborators, James Harris and Charles Jennens, than to Milton. They had the good sense to eliminate many of the most Miltonian elements of the two poems—musically improbable lines from "L'Allegro," such as:

> Hard by, a cottage chimney smokes,
> From betwixt two aged oaks,
> Where Corydon and Thyrsis met,
> Are at their savoury dinner set
> Of herbs, and other country messes,
> Which the neat-handed Phyllis dresses;
> And then in haste her bow'r she leaves,
> With Thestylis to bind the sheaves;
> Or if the earlier season lead
> To the tann'd haycock in the mead.

On the other hand, Handel's collaborators repeat in recitative perhaps the trashiest line in the entire poem multiple times: "And if I give thee honour due/Mirth, admit thee of thy crew." They do it not because they thought it was a great lyric, but because it makes a useful way for the cheerful character to reclaim the ongoing discourse from the thoughtful one. What remains of the original texts consists of pastoral imagery in the first part, urban in the second, most of it pretty generic. What is not generic, however, is Handel's music. Consider the aria "Sweet bird." Handel produced lots of "bird" arias, but this one may be the longest that he ever wrote (up to fifteen minutes in some performances), with the voice and solo flute vying for supremacy in an extravaganza of chirping and twittering ornamentation.

Milton has little to do with this, as he also has no involvement at all with the third part, "The Moderate Man." This was supposedly added at Handel's request to round out and resolve the conflict in the first two parts, and critics have taken Jennens to task for his own modest literary efforts. After all, nothing is duller in music than an excess of moderation. We needn't have worried. Handel reserved for this section, the briefest of the three, his very greatest duet, "As steals the morn," with the words based on Shakespeare—not that this matters particularly, either. It's the softly pulsating strings, the lyrical solos for oboe and bassoon, and the ecstatically soaring vocal lines that engage the listener's sympathy.

Of course there are splendid phrases taken from Milton throughout; I am thinking now of the magnificent solo with chorus in part 2, "Populous cities please me then," but let's be fair and "give the honor due" to Handel, Harris, and Jennens for a collaboration that took two relatively unwieldy poems and fashioned them into a vehicle that set the composer's genius alight.

Finally, you may well be wondering what *L'Allegro, il Penseroso ed il Moderato* is "about." The answer, which accounts for the work's special place in Handel's output, is simple: pleasure. This is pretty far from Milton's usual concerns, but it suits Handel perfectly. The last lines of the whole work say it best: "Thy pleasures, Moderation, give/In them alone we truly live." Handel sets himself the enjoyable task of illustrating the various pleasures of cheerfulness, thoughtfulness, and at last, moderation in all things.

Now Handel was not himself known for his moderate qualities. This may account for the minor key of the closing chorus; but pleasure he could and would describe. The classical imagery and freedom from specifically Christian doctrinal content permitted him to exalt the subject of pleasure with an uninhibited directness found nowhere else in his non-operatic vocal works. That makes *L'Allegro* a uniquely important and captivating personal statement.

The moral allegory that characterizes *The Choice of Hercules* returns in Handel's first, middle, and last oratorio, *The Triumph of Time and Truth*. Its most famous aria, "Lascia la spina," which became one of Handel's greatest hits when transplanted to *Rinaldo* as "Lascia ch'io pianga," is discussed in detail in chapter 7. His affection for this, his first oratorio, was extraordinary and understandable. In the original Italian version of 1707 there were only four characters (Beauty, Pleasure, Counsel, and Time), and no chorus. The soloists sing an unbroken chain of arias, many staggeringly virtuosic and beautiful. For many Handel fans, this remains the version of choice, both for its freshness as well as its conceptual clarity.

The version of 1737, with the rather abstruse *disinganno* (literally, "undeceit") of the title changed to the more direct *verità* ("truth"), was cobbled together when Handel was transitioning from opera to— something else. He still wasn't quite sure what that "something else" ought to be, and the result is a multimedia extravaganza with added choruses, an organ concerto or two, a sonata for solo carillon, and much else besides. It's very long and the score was only recently reassembled and recorded, quite well, for Naxos. This "new and improved" version was, evidently, successful, but Handel let it drop from his repertoire when he turned decisively toward English oratorio.

Finally, at the very end of his life, Handel returned to the work, fitting English words to the original music, and adapting new numbers as necessary. There is some question as to how direct his involvement actually was. By this time he was totally blind, and his health was failing, but there can be little doubt that he sanctioned the final result. In this last version, in addition to the generous fund of pastoral imagery ("Dryads, sylvan, with fair Flora," "Pleasure's gentle Zephyrs playing," "On the valleys," etc.), we can't help but be struck by the emphasis on images of the inexorable passing of time. The very first chorus, "Time is supreme," makes the point with singular directness and clarity.

However, it is Beauty's concluding aria, with its main theme and texture so prophetic of Bach's famous *Air [on the G-string]*, now scored for strings and solo oboe, that lingers most in the memory:

> Guardian angels, oh, protect me,
> And in Virtue's path direct me,
> While resigned to Heaven above,
> Let no more this world deceive me,
> Nor let idle passions grieve me,
> Strong in faith, in hope, in love.

It may not be great poetry, but it would be difficult to imagine any artist leaving us with more decent and humane words of farewell. Here, it seems to me, we find the reason and justification for Handel's return to this music at very end of his life. If the result may not be, of necessity, one of his greatest works, it remains one of his most moving.

Choral Characterization

It might surprise you to learn that the "Hallelujah" in *Messiah* was not Handel's favorite chorus. According to historical sources, that honor goes to "He saw the lovely youth," the second act finale in *Theodora*. It is easy to understand the reason for Handel's choice. After all, he wrote many "Hallelujah"s, but "He saw the lovely youth" is definitely distinctive, beginning with a solemn Largo and gradually working its way, through steadily increasing tempo and by way of a splendid fugue, to a warmly satisfying climax. No trumpets and drums here: just richly textured vocal polyphony and a strongly optimistic assertion of faith.

On the other hand, a number of Handel scholars rank as his greatest single chorus the epic "How dark, o Lord, are They decrees" from *Jephtha*, both for its scale—at more than eight minutes, it is one of Handel's longest choruses—as well as its harmonic audacity and tragic sentiment. Again, there is no questioning the music's power or quality. Also unusual is the resigned fatalism of the text:

No certain bliss,
No solid peace
We mortals know
On earth below.
Yet on this maxim still obey:
Whatever is, is right.

This is about as far from "Hallelujah" as it's possible to get, musically as well as philosophically. The music stands as a testament to Handel's feeling for dramatic truth in word setting.

For many listeners, Handel *is* his choruses. If you grew up and started collecting records in the 1950s or '60s, you most likely heard selections of choral music from the oratorios sung by groups such as the Mormon Tabernacle Choir, the Robert Shaw Chorale, or your local oratorio society or church choir. Performances of complete works beyond *Messiah* or *Israel in Egypt* were rare, and in the event, stylistically anachronistic. The emphasis would always be on the more uplifting, spiritual pieces, of the "Hallelujah" and "Praise the Lord" variety. Such programs, enjoyable though they might be, scarcely did justice to Handel's genius as a choral composer because it fell to him to do more than merely sing God's praises to the thunderous sound of dozens, hundreds, or even thousands of massed voices.

In the chorus, Handel discovered an entirely new way to create and portray *character* in music, the distinctive personality of the crowd, be they Israelites, pagans, Christians, virgins, warriors, Egyptians, Babylonians, Philistines—you name it. To each he gave a musical idiom specific to the dramatic context, and in so doing he set a standard for all future composers not just of oratorio, but also of opera. It would be difficult to imagine the gigantic crowd scenes in French grand opera and its offspring, from Verdi's *Aida* to Wagner's Knights of the Holy Grail, absent Handel's prior demonstration of the potentialities of the chorus.

This discovery was not entirely new. Already in one of the very first operas, Monteverdi's *Orfeo* of 1607, we find the chorus participating fully in the story, but over the course of the seventeenth century, Italian opera and oratorio increasingly became the exclusive preserve of the solo singer. Handel's practice, then, might more properly be called a rediscovery. What was truly original, however, was Handel's sovereign mastery of choral characterization within the medium of the oratorio, coupled with the fact that he was the first great composer whose music never disappeared from the active repertoire—even if this represented only a tiny fraction of his complete output. His choral writing served as a model: in short, as a *classic*.

It is very interesting to chart the evolution of Handel's increasingly flexible treatment of the chorus through his first oratorios. Already in *Esther* we find an ensemble of Persian soldiers opposed to the expected chorus of Israelites. The Persians in this case act as a communal extension of "bad guy" Haman's murderous intentions. In the next work, *Deborah*, the balance has shifted. The High Priest of Baal is a minor role and the chorus has become the principal voice of the Baal worshipers, as well as a full participant in the action. For *Athalia*, Handel and his librettist divide the choral "characters" into various subgroups, thereby encouraging a more varied and colorful treatment of vocal texture:

Israelite
Chorus of Young Virgins
Chorus of Israelites
Chorus of Priests and Levites

Baal Worshipers
Chorus of Attendants
Chorus of Sidonian Priests

At this point, Handel was ready to attempt his most radical experiment in choral characterization: *Israel in Egypt*, where, as the title suggests, the chorus assumes not just the principal role, it's the only role. As a clinic displaying just about everything that a composer can do with massed voices, the work has no peer either in Handel's output or anyone else's. At the same time (1739), Handel produced one of his greatest masterpieces, *Saul*, in which the chorus features both as a participant in the action and, in numbers, such as "Envy, eldest born of hell," as a commentator in the ancient Greek sense. Most of the choruses in *Messiah* and *Solomon* ("May no rash intruder," "Praise the Lord with harp and tongue!") function similarly, even if the latter work differentiates the various choral groupings as Priests, Israelites, and so forth.

Undoubtedly Handel's most sophisticated exercise in choral characterization occurs in *Belshazzar,* where the massed voices have no less than four independent roles: the pleasure-loving Babylonians, the conquering Persians, the captive Jews, and as choral commentary. Here is the order in which they appear throughout the work:

Babylonians: "Behold, by Persia's hero made"

Chorus: "All empires upon God depend"

Chorus: "Sing, oh ye heav'ns!"

Jews: "Recall, oh king! thy rash command"

Jews: "By slow degrees the wrath of God"

Chorus and Semi-Chorus: "See, from his post Euphrates flies!"

Persians: "To arms, to arms!"

Babylonians: "Ye tutelar gods of our empire, look down"

Babylonians: "Oh dire portentous sight!"

Babylonian Wise Men: "Alas! too hard a task the king imposes"

Babylonians: "Oh misery!—oh terror!"

Chorus: "Oh glorious prince!"

Jews: "Bel boweth down"

Soli and Chorus: "Tell it out among the heathen"

Soli and Chorus: "I will magnify thee"

As you can see, this is a very large assignment, and it falls between an extensive storyline of betrayal, conquest, and divine judgment involving Belshazzar; his mother, Nitocris; the Persian king, Cyrus; the biblical prophet, Daniel; and Gobrias, an Assyrian ally of Cyrus. And of course, you get the epic scene featuring the hand of God writing on the wall during the great feast of the Babylonians. *Belshazzar*, in case you haven't guessed, is a long work, running about three hours in total. The Babylonians are generally light-hearted and love to party; the Persians provide the military element with trumpets and timpani, the Jews are humble and subdued until the end, whereas the big "Greek" choruses give Handel a chance to indulge his taste for counterpoint and build his most monumental musical structures. The whole is a tour de force in the composer's most powerful, dramatic style.

The list of choruses above gives not just a sense of the range of characterization that Handel demands, but also some of the musical means at his disposal both here and in his other oratorios. There are numbers that subdivide the larger ensemble into "semichoruses" (often by sex), or small groups to portray additional characters (the wise men of Babylon, or the Chorus of Virgins in *Samson*). Other pieces feature some or all of the soloists in alternation with the choir, a thrilling effect often reserved for the ends of acts. You can sample the former on the accompanying disc in "Welcome, welcome mighty king!" from *Saul*, and the latter in the excerpt from *Judas Maccabaeus*. Just about the only thing not present in *Belshazzar* is Handel's use of the massively textured double chorus, in eight parts, such as we find in *Deborah*, *Israel in Egypt*, and *Solomon*.

Handel's choral writing added an extra musical dimension to the oratorios that is largely missing from the operas, compensating to some extent for the absence of visual spectacle. The sheer "bigness" of these pieces offered concert promoters the chance to entice audiences with a lavish entertainment at a fraction of the cost of staged musical drama. If opera remained largely a show for the wealthy, oratorios on biblical subjects that everyone could be expected to know gave the culturally ambitious middle classes a medium of their own, while the presence of the chorus further "democratized" the experience. Given these factors it's not surprising, looking back in hindsight, that it was these great choral works that secured Handel's reputation for posterity.

Two English Operas

One of the advantages to looking at the large list of works at the head of this chapter is the fact that we can see clearly that although works on biblical subjects predominate, the entire corpus of oratorios and oratorio-like compositions contains a very substantial amount of music on other themes as well. And so in 1744/5, mixed in with work on *Joseph and His Brethren* and *Belshazzar*, we find two English operas, *Semele* and *Hercules*, settings of stories taken from Greek mythology.

There is, actually, some controversy over whether these two works deserve to be called operas at all, seeing as how they were not intended to be staged, and include choral participation (not as much as in the biblical oratorios but still substantial by contemporary operatic standards). No doubt they could be produced in full theatrical regalia—indeed in modern times they have been, quite successfully—but much of the dispute comes down to quibbling over technicalities. As far as I am concerned, if it looks like an opera and screams like an opera, it's an opera. The presence of the chorus is no more disqualifying than it is in Verdi's *Aida* or, perhaps more pertinently, Britten's *Peter Grimes*.

In other words, as operas in English, they constitute the first flowering of a current that had to wait until the twentieth century before it really began to flow. In this respect Handel was far, far ahead of his time. It also doesn't hurt that we now regard *Semele* and *Hercules* as two of his finest works in any medium, not because they are English operas, but because they contain two of his most convincing and powerful female character portraits: the hedonistic narcissist Semele herself, and Hercules's jealous wife, Dejanira. In case you haven't noticed, most of the best operatic roles, even from the baroque period when castratos were all the rage, go to the principal women characters. The title of *Semele* speaks for itself, while that of *Hercules* could, with more justice, have been called *Dejanira*.[7]

Neither work was particularly successful in Handel's lifetime. It seems he was being actively sabotaged by the rival "opera of the nobility," for which he had refused to compose and which was on the verge of financial collapse. Under the circumstances the production of two new "operas in all but name" was viewed, with good reason, as a provocation, particularly as it was well known that he never shied away from a fight. Still, Handel partisans and the performers themselves recognized the quality of the music. The fact that the two pieces enjoyed only very limited runs in the composer's lifetime may well have proved fortunate for posterity, as both have come down to us intact as regards their original conceptions.

Semele is Handel's most unabashed tribute to the joys of love and sexual pleasure. It probably helps that the libretto was based on an earlier play not by a clergyman, but by Restoration playwright and poet William Congreve (author of two sayings that have come down to us as, "Music has charms to soothe the savage breast," and the famous paraphrase "Hell hath no fury like a woman scorned"). The main thread of the plot concerns the god Jupiter's infatuation with the lovely, self-absorbed, defiantly nymphomaniacal, none-too-bright Semele, who gets tricked by Jupiter's jealous wife, Juno, into demanding that her lover appear in his lethal (to mortals) divine form. This he does, having foolishly promised to grant Semele any wish, and she's promptly reduced to ashes out of which Bacchus, the god of wine and frat parties, arises to put uninhibited merriment on a more permanent basis. The final chorus tells the whole story:

> Happy, happy shall we be,
> Free from care, from sorrow free.
> Guiltless pleasures we'll enjoy,
> Virtuous love will never cloy;
> All that's good and just we'll prove,
> And Bacchus crown the joys of love.

Despite the fact that Semele winds up as toast, the piece is more satirical comedy than anything else. Her famous aria "Myself I shall adore" (sung into a mirror) speaks eloquently of the situation, whereas Juno's celebration of Semele's demise, "Above measure is the pleasure that my revenge supplies," has got to be the most deliciously bitchy solo in the entire repertoire. Other famous numbers include act 1's final aria with chorus "Endless pleasure, endless love," Jupiter's "Where'er you walk," and Juno's exciting "Iris, hence away!"—the latter popularized by mezzo-soprano Marilyn Horne, and a standout item on many modern Handel recitals. There is a stupendous recording of the complete work on Deutsche Grammophon featuring Horne (as Juno and Semele's sister Ino), John Aler (Jupiter), and Kathleen Battle perfectly cast as Semele, all under the direction of John Nelson.

If the theme of jealousy plays a prominent role in *Semele*, it is overwhelmingly the subject of *Hercules*. Indeed, jealousy is a topic that occurs frequently in Handel; one that he always treated with great power and psychological insight. In this respect, *Hercules* might be seen as a sort of secular counterpart to *Saul*. Both works feature major "jealousy" choruses: in *Hercules* it's "Jealousy! Infernal pest"; and in *Saul* we find "Envy, eldest born of hell," both in their respective work's second acts. In each, the main character's love, driven by jealousy, turns to murderous rage and madness.

There's a bit of backstory to *Hercules* that it helps to know. In Greek mythology, Hercules encounters the centaur Nessus attempting to force himself on Dejanira. Enraged, Hercules kills Nessus by shooting him with an arrow, and as he dies the centaur tells Dejanira that his blood will make Hercules love her forever. In reality, the blood is poison that will cause whoever it touches to die in excruciating agony. Dejanira, too easily fooled, smears the blood on a cloak and keeps it handy, just in case.

When the opera begins, Hercules has been away in battle for a year and Dejanira despairs of his safe return. He does come back, however, victorious and with the captive and very beautiful Princess Iole as prisoner. Dejanira immediately assumes the worst. Her jealousy evolves in six arias, one duet (with Iole), and a concluding mad scene, "Where shall I fly?" that is one of the very greatest moments in all of opera and the first in a long line of "crazy lady" characterizations—everything from Lucia's role in *Lucia di Lammermoor* to Verdi's Lady Macbeth and the Kostelnička in Janáček's *Jenůfa*—on which innumerable musical careers have been built.

Dejanira's mad scene immediately follows the equally remarkable depiction of Hercules's death. Handel marks them both simply "accompagnato," that is, accompanied recitative, because there were no terms available to describe exactly what he was doing. Obviously a formal, da capo aria would have been a wildly inappropriate way to depict Hercules's death agony or Dejanira's descent into madness, and so in each case Handel creates his own form based on the dictates of the text. Dejanira's *scena*, for example, following her introductory exclamations of horror, takes the form ABABCACA.

The words are wonderful. Who knew that there was an adjectival form of "snakes," as is the "snakey whips" borne by the vengeful Furies that Dejanira imagines are out to punish her? The "C" portion of the scene consists of the line "Alas, no rest the guilty find, from the pursuing Furies of the mind." Handel's vertiginous coloratura no longer expresses mere virtuosity: it is a graphic depiction of Dejanira's inner turmoil and mental instability. In the hands of a great singing actress this music is devastating, and it has become a popular recital item in concert and on recordings. You can hear it magnificently performed by Joyce DiDonato on her Handel recital *Furore*, (Warner/Virgin Classics) along with two other of Dejanira's arias—"There in myrtle shades reclined" and "Cease, ruler of the day, to rise." She also appears in a video of the complete work (Naxos).

Hercules has been recorded more frequently than *Semele*, perhaps because it's a straightforward tragedy and thus the more obviously serious of the two works. It's also a bit shorter. *Hercules*'s two most important recordings, conducted by John Eliot Gardiner and Marc Minkowski, both appeared on the Archiv label. Minkowski's features a really excellent Dejanira from Anne Sophie von Otter, although Sarah Walker, for Gardiner, is pretty impressive too. Gardiner also has the better title character in bass John Tomlinson, but either performance represents the piece very well.

You might say that the relationship between Handel's two great English operas is similar to that between Mozart's *Don Giovanni* and *Così fan tutte*—the one darkly passionate and more obviously dramatic, with the other's psychological depths hidden under a veneer of studied frivolity. The characters in *Hercules* are also more relatable than the gods and goddesses in *Semele*, whose title character herself is hardly conventionally appealing. That said, there's a sensuous quality to the music of *Semele* that represents one of Handel's greatest expressive gifts, and he never had another opportunity to indulge it as lavishly as he does here.

The New Testament

La Resurrezione (1708)
Brockes Passion (1719)
Messiah (1742)
Theodora (1750)

Handel was, by all accounts, a sincerely religious man, even if he kept his beliefs private and may not have held conventional views on the subject. Had he remained in Germany he doubtless would have become, like Bach and Telemann, a composer primarily for the Lutheran Church. As we all know, it didn't work out that way, and so we face the remarkable fact that, aside from a few apprentice works, Handel wrote nothing of significance for his own denomination. All of his mature liturgical music was composed either in Italy, for the Catholic rite, or for the Church of England. This bothered Handel not a whit, and despite what must have been a certain amount of pressure at various times, he steadfastly retained his original Lutheran faith, quietly, and above all privately.

Liturgical music aside, there are four concert oratorios that treat New Testament themes, and these do represent and admirably embody the three Christian cultures in which Handel worked: Germany, Italy, and England, and so Lutheran, Catholic, and Anglican. Only one, *Messiah*, has achieved anything like the popularity it deserves, and it has already been discussed. The other three, despite that fact that they all contain much excellent music, remain among Handel's least-known major works. It's a curious state of affairs and it pays to look into the possible reasons more closely.

The first point to keep in mind is that nonliturgical music on New Testament themes generally, in Handel's day, needed to be approached with great care. Popular as it was, the theater still had a reputation as a sinkhole of sin and depravity, largely due to the participation of women—as if having men singing female characters was somehow less morally suspect. As we have already seen, Handel's theatrical works, whether operas or oratorios, constitute a veritable fiesta of sexual ambiguity in this respect, with men singing women, women singing men, castratos, countertenors, and what have you. Whole books have been written about the topic.

For our purposes, it suffices to note that while dramatically exciting Old Testament subjects could, as long as they were not actually staged, escape the moral taint of the theater—even to the point where *Solomon* could be conceived as a (female) contralto role—Christian stories remained largely off limits. Remember that *Messiah* had an indifferent reception at its first London performances due to questions about its appropriateness as an "entertainment." We have already seen how the pope sanctioned Handel's patron in Rome, the Marchese Ruspoli, for performing *La Resurrezione* with a female singer as Mary Magdalene.

This antitheatrical prejudice was no joke. It remained a cultural tradition manifesting in various degrees of censorship well into the twentieth century. Even those lavish Hollywood bible extravaganzas of the 1950s and '60s cautiously represented the character of Jesus only by a pair of sandaled feet, any attempt at a more realistic presentation being considered offensive. *Ben Hur* may be subtitled *A Tale of the Christ*, but we never actually get to see all of Him. His feet (and a few other body parts) were played by Claude Heater, an uncredited extra.

The three big oratorios treating the life of Jesus from some angle thus do so obliquely, in keeping with local custom. *La Resurrezione* really is an opera in all but name, virtually indistinguishable from the genuine article, and a transparent effort to evade the papal ban on operatic performances in Rome. Its plot may be minimal, and the characterization sketchy—except for the juicy role of Lucifer, of course—but the fact that Handel later reused much of its material in operas from *Agrippina* to *Giulio Cesare* is very telling. The arias, whether flashy or soulful, could be adapted to multiple contexts and purposes.

This same observation also applies to the Brockes Passion, which Handel wrote around 1717, allegedly for performance in Hamburg. Barthold Heinrich Brockes's text is a mash-up of the four Gospel stories, including the Last Supper, the betrayal of Jesus, and the Crucifixion, interspersed with a few choruses, some chorales, and a huge number of solos from allegorical characters such as the Daughter of Zion and the Faithful Souls. Jesus himself actually gets to sing some arias and a couple of duets, though the role is not large relatively speaking. There is no extensive biblical quotation, as opposed to Bach's Gospel-specific Passions, the St. Matthew and St. John, pointing the poem's status as an independent spiritual but still nonliturgical work. Its formal title, *Der für die Sünde der Welt gemarterte und sterbende Jesus* ("Jesus Suffering Martyrdom and Dying for the Sins of the World"), explains why everyone calls it the Brockes Passion, even in Germany.

Brockes's text turned out to be hugely popular. It was set by more than a dozen major German composers of the day, including Handel's friend Telemann, whose contemporaneous version is arguably the best of the lot. This embarrassment of riches allowed local musical societies to assemble "greatest hits" versions of the work, taking a bit from each composer. Handel's setting was widely pirated in this fashion, and not just by Bach. The full poem contains 117 numbers ranging in length from a few seconds of recitative to full-fledged arias (Handel's version requires "only" 106 and still lasts a good two and a half hours). If history has decided that two German Passion settings, both by Bach, are more than enough for posterity you can hear plenty of the Brockes Passion spread out over the Chandos Anthems, *Esther, Deborah, Athalia*, and even the opera *Radamisto*.

The Brockes Passion has been undervalued by English Handel scholars, perhaps not surprisingly in light of the composer's subsequent achievement. Both performances and recordings have been comparatively rare. It's certainly true that the large number of contemplative arias for allegorical characters, such as the Daughter of Zion, makes for a singularly undramatic retelling of what can be an extremely gripping (and gory) tale, but these arias also contain most of the best music, as Handel well knew when he chose to insert them into later works. It's always worth emphasizing that this practice does not reflect laziness as much as it does musical aptness. A composer of Handel's gifts could as easily write a new piece as adapt an older one, and so his faith in the music of his single Passion setting speaks volumes.

The very specific local circumstances governing the form and content of *La Resurrezione* and the Brockes Passion suggest that Handel may initially have considered them, at least to an extent, as repositories of music for future use. Just the opposite is true of his favorite oratorio, *Theodora*. The work contains almost no borrowings at all, and because it was composed at the end of his career, it was never quarried for material later on. There are no doctrinal issues either. The plot is a straightforward tale of love and sacrifice in a setting that happens coincidentally to be Christian, but it could have involved any two conflicting cultures or religions. Handel's focus remains squarely on the main, very human characters. There are no allegorical, divine, or otherwise mystical participants.

Theodora is, in other words, drama plain and simple. Its historical neglect is as inexplicable as the music is gorgeous. In recent times, the oratorio has made a major comeback, both in the theater and in more than half a dozen recordings. The title character is one of those plum roles on which a fine mezzo soprano who specializes in expressing noble suffering can build a career. Indeed, the late, great Lorraine Hunt Lieberson had notable successes in various productions either as Theodora or her friend Irene. She appears in these roles on complete recordings, and she regularly sang selected arias in concert and on disc ("Angels, ever bright and fair," "With Darkness, deep," "Oh! that I on wings could rise," "As with rosy steps the morn," "Defend her Heav'n," to name a few).

The failure of *Theodora* in Handel's day resulted in one of this most memorable, if possibly apocryphal, quips: "The Jews won't come because it is a Christian story, and the ladies won't come because it is a virtuous one." For its vivid characterization and human qualities, then, *Theodora* remains the most moving of all of Handel's theatrical works on Christian themes. Unlike *La Resurrezione* and the Brockes Passion, it preaches no doctrine; and unlike *Messiah*, it can't be chopped up and arranged to suit a particular holiday. Like any good story it needs to be taken in whole, but its principal themes of love, sacrifice, and redemption arguably make it the most archetypically Christian work of them all.

What To Do During Intermission (Concertos and Orchestral Music)

Overtures
Concerti Grossi Opp. 3 and 6
Organ Concertos
Concerto in *Alexander's Feast*
Concerti a due cori

Handel wrote virtually no free-standing orchestral music. It all was composed for a specific purpose or occasion. Even his most famous set of concertos, the twelve works in Op. 6, turned up in his theatrical performances in whole or in part.

The close relationship between the orchestral music and operas and oratorios was for a long time obscured by the fact that, in order to understand it, you had to really know your Handel. It's not just anyone who can appreciate the fact, for example, that the closing chorus in part 1 of *La Resurrezione*, "Il Nume vincitor" ("Victorious God"), returns as the final number (the Bourrée) of the *Water Music*'s Second Suite (in D major). For that, you need to live, breathe, and die Handel, as many of today's scholars do. Thanks to their work, and its unprecedented accessibility via publishing, recordings, and the Internet, we now know more than ever before about how Handel's orchestral music fits into the wider context of his musical activity more generally.

You certainly don't need to absorb any of these details in order to enjoy this music for its own sake, exactly as listeners the world over have done for centuries. There's no quiz coming up later. I believe the knowledge is valuable, however, for the opportunity it offers to break down the traditional barriers between orchestral and vocal music—a dichotomy that arose during the nineteenth century—and see Handel's output as the remarkably seamless whole that it really is. So, let's start with a very brief discussion of how we got where we are.

The distinction between composers who appeared to specialize in vocal versus instrumental music arose as a result of the triumph of Viennese classicism at the end of the eighteenth century. Haydn and Beethoven were, relatively speaking, failures as opera composers (Mozart could do anything), and the vocal medium was in any case heading in the direction of *opera buffa*, or comedy. Serious music was instrumental—the symphony and string quartet—which had the advantage of not being as obviously based on Italian norms. The rise of nationalism as a cultural force only enhanced the desirability of finding indigenous musical forms; and so, starting in Germany and spreading outward like waves in a pond, the appeal of instrumental music grew from place to place, gathering force as empires and kingdoms became countries and nations.

There was a moral component to this as well. Instrumental music was "pure," unsullied by the taint of the theater. Never mind that most composers still spent most of their time writing vocal works. As long as they stuck to songs or church music and avoided opera (or were really bad at it), their reputation remained secure. The argument for the superiority of instrumental music was, as I hope you can see, very elitist and theoretical. Most people, when they thought of music at all, had songs in mind, and they still do—everywhere, that is, except in the twilight zone known as the universe of classical music. That's why such shows as *American Idol* involve singers and not pianists or string quartets. This is also why, today at least, there is a pretty clear line of demarcation in the world of classical music between opera or choral music fans, and everyone else.

In Handel's day, the human voice still reigned supreme. Musical instruments offered but pale imitations of the art of singing. The forms of vocal and instrumental music were pretty much identical, and because Handel was Handel, his orchestral works show this unusually clearly. If a concerto wasn't musically related to a specific vocal piece, then it probably served as an added attraction in between the acts of one. Indeed, we see the beginnings of the fondness for purely instrumental pieces in the fact that Handel quickly realized that performing an organ concerto during intermission was an added draw. Probably no one was as surprised as he was at the popularity of these "mixed-media" events; but as long as the formula worked, he went for it.

Then again, when we consider the circumstances of a night at the theater in Handel's day, his actions make a lot more sense. No one was expected to sit still for three or four hours and concentrate on the stage. People came and went at will; they chatted and socialized. The lights remained on throughout—after all, you needed what was effectively a fire extinguisher to turn them off. There was no orchestra pit. The musicians sat at floor level, their parts illuminated by candles. If you wanted, you could take a walk on stage to see what was happening— preferably at intermission, but you never know. The evening's featured entertainment had to compete with whatever else happened to be going on in the auditorium. Capturing and holding the audience's attention was a major task. In short, it was a circus.

Handel's largest single body of orchestral music consists of the overtures, sinfonias, and interludes used in the operas, oratorios, and other large vocal works. Many were published in sets of parts during his lifetime, and at least sixty overtures were arranged for keyboard so that they could be played at home. Two of his most popular instrumental pieces, the "Pastoral Symphony" from *Messiah* and "The Arrival of the Queen of Sheba" from *Solomon*, fall into this general category. Handel also mined his overtures, or bits of them if they had multiple sections, as concerto movements, just as he transferred arias from one work to the next. The provenance of the Six Concerti Grossi, Op. 3 reveals this procedure at work quite graphically.

John Walsh, Handel's publisher, issued Op. 3 with, it seems, little initial participation from the composer. Originally it contained a work, now known as No. 4b, not by Handel at all. Evidence that he ultimately had something to do with the publication consists in the fact that No. 4b was later replaced by Concerto No. 4a, which is indisputably Handel's own. A concerto grosso consists of any number of solo instruments contrasting with the full orchestra, usually strings plus continuo. Typically for Handel, there is otherwise no standard form. Indeed, anything from the baroque era that was not specifically designated as part of an overture or suite became a potential concerto movement more or less by default, simply because the musical texture invariably featured a continuo accompaniment with the tune—the solo lines—on top.

Concerto No. 1 is richly scored for two recorders, two oboes, and two bassoons (plus strings and continuo, which we can take for granted from here on). It has three movements and appears to contain no obvious borrowings. The first and third movements of the five-part Concerto No. 2, however, scored for two oboes and one bassoon, derive from instrumental music in the Brockes Passion. The first three movements of Concerto No. 3, for oboe (or flute) and bassoon, come from the Chandos Anthem "My song shall be alway" and the Chandos Te Deum. Only the finale is unrelated to a vocal work. Concerto No. 4a, for two oboes and bassoon, served as intermission music or a "second overture" at a benefit performance of Handel's opera *Amadigi* given on June 20, 1716. The first, second, and fourth (of five) movements in Concerto No. 5 were also taken from Chandos Anthems: "In the Lord put I my trust" and "As pants the hart." The scoring is also for two oboes and bassoon.

Concerto No. 6 has a very tortured history. As printed originally it contained only two movements, scored for flute, two oboes, organ, and bassoon. The first movement comes from Handel's opera *Ottone*, whereas the finale, with solo organ, first turned up at the end of the monstrously long, multimovement overture to *Il pastor fido* (1712). Many recorded performances diddle this concerto to add a slow movement from elsewhere, and some even replace the finale. Whatever the solution, you can plainly see that Handel's vocal works, both sacred and secular, have left their fingerprints all over these concertos.

If questions about the composer's involvement in the publication of Op. 3 cast some doubt on his intentions in using so much material from the vocal works, the circumstances surrounding the appearance of the Twelve Grand Concertos, Op. 6 only confirm our original suppositions. Handel personally supervised the release of these pieces, and as I note in discussing the First Concerto in chapter 7, his procedure here was exactly the same. We find a similar mix of new and adapted material, and even more than in Op. 3 Handel found these works to be very handy as interludes between the acts of his oratorio performances—that is, useful both as additional entertainment and doubtless as advertisements for the newly issued complete set of concertos.

With the popularity of his orchestral music an established fact, Handel proceeded to take maximum advantage in his organ concertos. This was a medium that he basically invented, and he was acknowledged as the greatest organist of his age. A concert in which he performed his own concertos offered his audience a considerable bonus in addition to the usual two and half hours or so of oratorio. Of the two major sets of six organ concertos (plus three additional works) that were eventually published as Opp. 4 and 7, the earlier Op. 4 group has solo parts that are a bit more fully written down. In Op. 7, Handel leaves whole movements, including adagios and fugues, to be improvised by the soloist. Today, sometimes they do and sometimes they don't, but if they don't there's plenty of miscellaneous Handel that can be used to fill in the blanks.

The Concerto Op. 4, No. 6 is, in fact, a harp concerto, deliciously scored with flutes and muted strings. Like Concerto Op. 4, No. 1, it was originally performed in *Alexander's Feast*—neither work to be confused with the actual "Concerto in *Alexander's Feast*," which is another piece entirely. Handel's Harp Concerto is the only eighteenth-century work for its solo instrument than anyone cares about today. The other concertos in the Op. 4 set were played alongside the oratorios *Esther* (Nos. 2 and 3), *Athalia* (No. 4), and *Deborah* (No. 5). Several movements in Op. 4 are arrangements from Handel's trio sonatas, but Concerto No. 2 enlarges upon the sinfonia that opens the lovely soprano motet *Silete venti*, while No. 4 contains an adaptation of a chorus in the opera *Alcina*.

We find the most telling relationship between Handel's orchestral and vocal works in his three Concerti a due cori, composed in the late 1740s. The very title, "Concerto with Two Choirs," makes the point especially clear. This was the period of the "Waratorios," and Handel had at his disposal a large orchestra with lots of woodwinds and brass. So, it only made sense that he would want to take advantage of these lavish forces by writing some virtuoso concertos for them to play alongside the larger works.

The first two concertos consist almost entirely of movements arranged from the earlier oratorios and operas—almost a "greatest hits" selection, or, it is tempting to think, perhaps a promotional effort. The Third Concerto was composed expressly for performance with *Judas Maccabaeus* and contains no borrowed music at all. These richly inventive pieces remain among Handel's least known orchestral works, for no good reason that I can find. It may be that the large forces that they require make them awkward to program for today's smaller-sized chamber orchestras and early music ensembles. Below, with a little help from the Halle Handel Critical Edition, I break down the concertos movement by movement so that you can see what Handel's sources were:

Concerto No. 1 in B-flat Major, HWV 332 "Concerto of Choruses"

1. Overture: Original, later adapted as the overture to *Alexander Balus*
2. Allegro ma non troppo: "And the glory of the Lord" (*Messiah*)
3. Allegro: "See from his post Euphrates flies" (*Belshazzar*)
4. Largo: Original, but based on the aria "S'io dir potessi" from *Ottone*
5. A tempo ordinario: "Lucky omens bless our rites" (*Semele*)
6. Alla breve moderato: "Attend the pair" (*Semele*)
7. Minuet: Original, but based on the aria "Non t'inganni la speranza" from *Lotario*

Concerto No. 2 in F Major, HWV 333

1. Pomposo: Aria "Jehova crown'd" (*Esther*)
2. Allegro: Chorus "He comes to end our woes" (*Esther*)
3. A tempo giusto: Chorus "Lift up your heads" (*Messiah*)
4. Largo: Chorus "Ye sons of Israel, mourn" (*Esther*)
5. Allegro ma non troppo: A mash up of music from the *Ode for the Birthday of Queen Anne* and a couple of arias from *Esther*
6. A tempo ordinario: Modeled on the chorus "God found them guilty" from *The Occasional Oratorio*

Concerto No. 3 in F Major, HWV 334: all new, written as an additional "draw" for performances of *Judas Maccabaeus*

Handel's concertos, one and all, are delightful pieces, tuneful, colorful, and easy on the ear. Most last between eight and twelve minutes, and reveal as much spontaneity and formal variety as anything else that he wrote. What makes them particularly remarkable is the fact that just by listening to and enjoying them, you acquire a window into the vocal works whose lives they share. You don't even have to be conscious of this aspect of the music; it just happens, and it's there for you if and when you're ready.

A *Pair* of Acis
Same Story, Different Music

Aci, Galatea e Polifemo (Serenata or Dramatic Cantata) 1708

Scoring: Flauto dolce [Recorder], Oboe, 2 Trumpets, Strings (Violins I, II, Violas, Cellos I, II, Basses), Continuo

Vocal Parts

Aci (soprano)
Galatea (alto)
Polifemo (bass)

Musical Numbers

Duet: Aci & Galatea "Sorge il di" ("Day breaks")

Recitative (Recit) & Aria: Galatea "Sforzano a piangere" ("Fate forces me to weep")

Recit & Aria: Acis "Che non può la gelosia" ("What can jealousy not achieve")

Recit: Acis & Galatea "Ma qual orrido suono" ("But what is that horrible sound")

Aria: Polifemo "Sibelar l'angui d'Aletto" ("The hissing of Alecto's snakes surrounds me")

Recit & Aria: Galatea "Benchè tuoni e l'età avampi" ("Your thunder and lightening do not scare me")

Recit & Aria: Polifemo "Non sempre, no, crudele" ("You will not always speak to me thus, cruel one")

Recit & Aria: Aci "Dell'aquila l'artigli" ("If the snake does not fear the eagle's talons")

Recit & Aria: Polifemo "Precipitoso nel mar" ("Falling rapidly into the sea")

Recit & Aria: Galatea "S'agita" ("Amidst the waves")

Recit & Trio: All Three "Proverà" ("She who will not accept my love")

Recit & Aria: Polifemo "Fra l'ombre e gl'orrori" ("From the shadows and horrors")

Recit & Aria: Aci "Qui l'augel" ("Here the bird flies happily from tree to tree")

Recit & Aria: Galatea "Se m'ami, o caro" ("If you love me, dear one, leave me")

Recit & Trio: All Three "Dolce amico" ("Dear and loving embrace")

Recit & Aria: Polifemo "Già và da balza in balza" ("The rock bounces back and forth")

Recit & Aria: Aci "O Dio, mio ben, soccorso!" ("Oh God, my love, help!")

Recit (Galatea & Polifemo) & Aria: Polifemo "Impara, ingrata" ("Learn, ingrate")

Recit & Aria: Galatea "Del mar fra l'onde" ("Amid the waves of the sea")

Recit: Polifemo "Ferma!" ("Stop!")

Trio: "Chi ben ama ha per oggetti" ("He who loves well has a goal")

Acis and Galatea (Variously called a Masque, Serenata, Oratorio, Pastoral Opera, Little Opera, etc) 1718

Scoring: Descant (Sopranino) Recorder/Piccolo, 2 Recorders/ Flutes, 2 Oboes, Strings (Violins I, II, Violas, Cellos, Basses), [Carillon], Continuo

Vocal Parts

Galatea (Soprano)
Acis (Tenor)
Damon (Tenor)
[Coridon (Tenor)]

Polyphemus (Bass)
Chorus

Musical Numbers

Act 1

Chorus: "Oh, the pleasure of the plains!"
Accompagnato: Galatea "Ye verdant plains and woody mountains"
Air: Galatea "Hush, ye pretty warbling quire!"
Air: Acis "Where shall I seek the charming fair?"
Recit & Air: Damon "Shepherd, what art thou pursuing?"
Recit & Air: Acis "Love in her eyes sits playing"
Recit & Air: "As when the dove"
Duet [& Chorus]: "Happy we"

Act 2

Chorus: "Wretched lovers!"
Accompagnato: Polyphemus "I rage, I melt, I burn"
Air: Polyphemus "O ruddier than the cherry"
Recit (Galatea & Polyphemus) & Air: Polyphemus "Cease to beauty to be suing"
Air: Damon "Would you gain the tender creature"
Recit & Air: Acis "Love sounds th' alarm"
Air: Damon "Consider, fond shepherd"
Recit & Trio (Acis, Galatea, Polyphemus): "The flocks shall leave the mountains"
Accompagnato: Acis "Help, Galatea! Help, ye parent gods!"
Chorus: "Mourn, all ye muses!"
Chorus & Galatea: "Must I my Acis still bemoan?"
Recit & Air: Galatea "Heart, the seat of soft delight"
Chorus: "Galatea, dry thy tears"

The tale of Acis and Galatea couldn't be simpler. Acis is a shepherd; Galatea, a sea nymph. They are happily in love. Polyphemus is a bullying Cyclops who has the hots for Galatea. When she rejects him, he grabs a boulder and crushes Acis to death in a jealous rage. The grieving Galatea, with a little help from Neptune, turns his remains into a spring flowing down to the sea so that she can join him forever. Polyphemus pouts.

Not the least wonderful thing about this most wonderful of composers is the fact that, even though these two works set the exact same story, and even though Handel invariably borrowed and adapted everything he could, they have nothing musically significant in common at all. Shocking, isn't it? Although it would be nice to be able to say that this state of affairs arose from some unfathomable long-range plan on Handel's part, the reality is probably somewhat more prosaic.

In the decade between the Italian and English language versions, 1708–18, Handel composed at least six operas:

- *Agrippina* (1709)
- *Rinaldo* (1711)
- *Il pastor fido* (1712)
- *Teseo* (1713)
- *Silla* (1713?)
- *Amadigi di Gaula* (1715)

That is a lot of work for which he needed a lot of music, and so he liberally raided his early serenata *Aci, Galatea e Polifemo*, spreading virtually the entire piece over the succeeding operas. It could be that by the time he came to write *Acis and Galatea* in 1718, he felt he had already used up much of his potential material. Although most of it is new, the English *Acis* is not entirely free from adaptations of earlier work—just not the Italian *Aci* (with a single trivial exception we don't need to discuss).

On the other hand, the fact that an aria from the Italian version ("Precipitoso nel mar") turns up—aptly—as "Swift inundation" in *Deborah* hints at the possibility that Handel did want to avoid mixing these particular apples and oranges. Indeed, he continued to use the serenata to fortify new works until, in 1732, disgusted by the growing popularity of the English piece in a host of unauthorized performances both professional and amateur, he decided to capitalize on his own success by jamming his *Aci* and *Acis* together with even more material in a bilingual, three-act mess that, not surprisingly, never quite caught on.

Undeterred, Handel continued to tinker with his pastoral "opera-torio," or whatever it is, for the rest of his life. Characters came and went. The shepherd Coridon, for example, only sings one aria and, like Damon, he's a tenor. His part was expendable. The final duet in act 1, "Happy we," gained a choral reprise, to which Handel even added a carillon part (you can hear it on Neville Marriner's Decca recording). The original serenata too continued to furnish material for the later operas and other vocal works, including *Atalanta* (1736) and *L'Allegro, il Penseroso ed il Moderato* (1740). Significantly, both of these works illustrate pastoral subjects, but *Joshua* (1748) certainly does not.

The shape in which *Acis and Galatea* usually gets performed today corresponds primarily to Handel's two-act revision of 1739. For those performances he gave the role of Damon to a boy soprano, for some reason, but the rest mostly remains as generally known. Unfortunately, the period instrument folks lately often have opted for some alleged, original 1718 version with minuscule forces, claiming scholarly sanction and with it a certain moral purity—this, despite the fact that Handel's first thoughts seem never to have been performed. It is very typical of the "authenticity" movement to proclaim the superiority of a conjectural modern restoration over what we know Handel actually did. The truth, of course, is that the main justification for such nonsense is financial, just as it was in his era.

While no one wants to revive his flagrantly opportunistic, bilingual pastiche edition of the score, there is no excuse for not presenting the version of the basic English text richest in musical color and variety. Everything that we know about Handel's own practice suggests that, in an ideal world, he would have done similarly. At the very least, the chorus should comprise more singers than just the soloists, and the instrumental ensemble should have a fair number of string players. *Acis and Galatea* is not a large work, but it shouldn't ever sound puny, monochrome, and thus expressively inhibited.

Both versions of the story run for about the same length: between 95 and 100 minutes on average; so you can readily see how sticking them together would have created easily a large work of standard operatic dimensions, even though Handel didn't use the entire serenata in 1732. Otherwise, they are very different. The whole point of this discussion is not to suggest that one is better than the other. Rather, comparison of the two illustrates how each remains fun to listen to in its own right,

and illuminates Handel's various strategies for creating a musical setting of the same plot in keeping with the individual circumstances and
conventions prevailing at the time.

The first thing to note, if you refer to the breakdown at the head of
this chapter, is that the two works feature very different voice types
for the role of Aci/Acis: soprano vs. tenor. Giving the character of the
Cyclops Polyphemus to a bass in both pieces was a no-brainer, but in the
serenata Aci is a soprano with a voice higher than that of Galatea! The
reason for this is complicated, but basically boils down to four factors:

1. The presence of superb soprano castrato singers. We'll have more to
   say about them in the next chapter.
2. The Italian baroque convention favoring high voices for heroes,
   mythical characters, gods, and young men.
3. The musical fact that high voices are, generally, the most agile, exciting, audible, and expressive.
4. Baroque music also, as we have seen, tended to organize music as
   a solo voice on top, with everything else down below as continuo
   accompaniment. This placed a natural emphasis on the soprano as
   the favored register, whether a person, a flute, or a violin.

As a result of these conventions, in Italian baroque dramatic music
there is absolutely no inherent relationship between the identity of the
character and the vocal register in which the male or female soloist
sings. The result may sound strange at first, but that's just the way it
was. For example, we happen to know the identities of the singers at the
first performances of *Aci, Galatea, e Polifemo*. At the premiere, Aci was
sung by a female soprano; Galatea, by a castrato. The second airing featured two castratos. In case you were wondering, Handel did compose
the role of Galatea for a female voice, but no one seems to have much
cared. All opera requires a certain willful suspension of disbelief; maybe
this convention demands an extra dose. Indeed, it's one of the hurdles
that baroque opera presents, but jumping it gets easier and easier.

Actually, modern listeners do catch a break: you will (hopefully)
never hear a male Galatea, and there haven't been too many male Acises,
either. This is because few of the current male falsettists who go by the
name of operatic "countertenors" have a true soprano range. They tend

to take heroic roles written for lower, heavier mezzo-soprano voices. As a result, in all of the available recordings of the Italian version, most of which are excellent, both Aci and Galatea are sung by women with, I should add, musically fabulous results. In the English *Acis* there are no such anomalies, aside from that odd surplus of tenors remedied by eliminating the part of Coridon and assigning his single aria, "Would you gain the tender creature," to Damon.

If you look at the orchestration of both pieces, you will note that they contain instrumentation characteristic of pastoral imagery: flutes and oboes primarily. Interestingly, the flutes (or recorders) tend to be associated with Galatea's texts speaking of waves and water: "S'agita in mezzo all' onde" ("Amidst the waves"), and in the English version there's the haunting transformation scene, where she sings:

> Heart, the seat of soft delight,
> Be thou now a fountain bright!
> Purple be no more thy blood,
> Glide thou like a crystal flood.
> Rock, thy hollow womb disclose!
> The bubbling fountain, lo! it flows;
> Through the plains he joys to rove,
> Murm'ring still his gentle love.

Polifemo has his proprietary instruments and scoring too, although in this case there are significant differences from 1708 to 1718. In the serenata, trumpets feature in the blustering aria "Sibelar l'angui d'Aletto," which is included on the accompanying CD and discussed in chapter 7. Most entertaining, though, is the freakishly mournful "Fra l'ombre e gl'orrori," with flute, muted violins, and double basses without cellos. The amusing gap between very high and very low instruments is a comic device that would endure from Haydn's "Clock" Symphony to Verdi's *Falstaff*, while the correspondingly insane vocal range, with leaps of two and half octaves, makes this giant as grotesque musically as any Cyclops must be physically.

The English *Acis*, on the other hand, finds Polyphemus accompanied by the piccolo or descant recorder in his lively comic aria "O ruddier than the cherry." This, too, is a bit of musical characterization that would reappear later, specifically in the person of the comically evil and equally licentious Monostatos from Mozart's *The Magic Flute*. Perhaps this is no coincidence. *Acis and Galatea* was one of several Handel works that Mozart arranged and reorchestrated for performances in Vienna. The piccolo also assumes its more normal, naturalistic job of evoking birdsong in Galatea's "Hush, ye pretty warbling quire!" You can see by Handel's treatment of the flute family in these two works how he exploits his ensemble in the most varied and colorful manner possible.

The character of Aci/Acis is less well developed than that of his costars if only for the reason that he has but two tasks: to express love for Galatea, and to get squashed by a boulder. He's a bit more prominent in the English piece because Polyphemus doesn't show up until the second act. However, considered purely as drama, the serenata actually has a more stage-worthy scenario than its successor because it dwells more completely on Galatea's rejection of Polifemo's advances, and hence on the motivations that give rise to the dramatic action. The Cyclops is a larger and more thoughtful (for an ogre) character in the earlier work, which has been produced successfully in the theater.

The English masque, by contrast, has a first act in which absolutely nothing happens, despite glorious music for Acis, Galatea, the worldly and sardonic shepherd Damon, and of course, the chorus. It's basically just a pastoral idyll in the Arcadian countryside, but what it lacks in dramatic force it more than makes up for in musical variety. The initial Sinfonia is delicious, and the concluding chorus, "Happy we," has got to be the giddiest thing that Handel ever wrote (and that's saying a lot). In act 2, the action speeds up considerably, with a powerful opening for the chorus, "Wretched lovers"; a quick and violent death for Acis; and then the obligatory lament for Galatea and her entourage.

Taken together, *Aci* and *Acis* offer the ideal gateway to Handel's large vocal works, the serenata to the Italian operas, the masque to the English odes and oratorios. In both cases you get a comprehensive sampling, only within a modest time frame perhaps more suitable to our hurried modern lives. The musical quality of Handel's early effort is attested to by the fact that he never ceased to reuse its arias in new contexts. The high repute of the English piece can be gleaned by noting that it was his most popular theatrical work during his lifetime, has never really left the repertoire, and was arranged by no less than Mozart and Mendelssohn.

One final point: the text of the English work, although not entirely securely attributed, seems mostly to have been the work of poets John Gay and Alexander Pope. It is certainly one of the most charming and, for poetry, directly comprehensible books that Handel ever set. This makes it especially easy for modern listeners to assimilate, even those who normally shy away from opera in English, or even opera generally. Gay would later go on almost to put Handel out of business when he produced *The Beggar's Opera*, but for this one moment, at least, "high" and "popular" art seemed to coexist in perfect harmony.

Sex and Drugs
and Da Capo Arias
The Operas

Handel Operas, with Recommended Recordings

Almira (1705)

Rodrigo (*Vincer se stesso è la maggior vittoria*) (1707)

—*Agrippina* (1709) [Gardiner/Decca or McGegan/Harmonia
   Mundi]

—*Rinaldo* (1711) [Jacobs/Harmonia Mundi or Hogwood/
   Decca]

Il pastor fido (1712)

Teseo (1713)

Silla (1713 probably)

Amadigi di Gaula (1715)

—*Radamisto* (1720) [McGegan/Harmonia Mundi or Curtis/
   Virgin (Warner)]

Muzio Scevola (1721: third act only)

Floridante (1721)

—*Ottone* (1723) [McGegan/Harmonia Mundi]

Flavio (1723)

—*Giulio Cesare* (1724) [Minkowski/Archiv or Jacobs/
   Harmonia Mundi]

—*Tamerlano* (1724) [Minasi/Naive]

—*Rodelinda* (1725) [Bolton/Farao (Video)]

Scipione (1726)

Alessandro (1726)

—*Admeto* (1727) [Curtis/Virgin Classics (Warner) or
    McGegan/Unitel (Video)]

Riccardo Primo (1727)

Siroe (1728)

Tolomeo (1728)

Lotario (1729)

—*Partenope* (1730) [Minasi/Erato]

Poro (1731)

Ezio (1732)

Sosarme (1732) [a.k.a. *Fernando*]

—*Orlando* (1733) [Jacobs/Archiv]

Arianna in Creta (1734)

Oreste (1734: Pasticcio)

—*Ariodante* (1735) [Minkowski/Archiv or Curtis/Virgin
    Classics (Warner)]

—*Alcina* (1735) [Christie/Erato or Curtis/Archiv]

Atalanta (1736)

Arminio (1737)

Giustino (1737)

Berenice (1737)

Faramondo (1738)

Alessandro Severo (1738: Pasticcio)

—*Serse* (*Xerxes*) (1738) [Christie/Virgin Classics (Warner)]

Giove in Argo (1739: Pasticcio)

Imeneo (1740)

Deidamia (1741)

The Handel Opera Revival: How It Really Happened

O pera is absurd.

It doesn't matter what kind we're discussing. The very idea of characters running around on stage singing either at one another or to themselves seems ridiculous; never mind what they're supposedly singing about, or what is theoretically happening to them while they're doing it. For some two centuries, Handel's operas were totally neglected because we were told that the aesthetic of baroque opera was obsolete. This presumes that the five hours of slow-motion, continuous orchestral philosophizing typical of, say, Wagnerian music drama is somehow more normal or legitimate than Handel's three hours of secco recitative and da capo arias. So, let's set the record straight. Nothing about opera is normal at any period, and therein resides its power to fascinate and to thrill.

Opera is also dangerous, and the danger only adds to its attractions. Its complexity as a theatrical medium is mind-boggling. Consider the need to hire, train and coordinate a conductor, orchestra, singers, chorus, stage extras, producer, prop makers, stagehands, costume and scenery designers—and don't think matters are any different now than they were two or three centuries ago. The number of things that can go wrong on any given night is near infinite. For that reason, on those still rare occasions when absolutely everything falls into place, the result is incomparable, going a long way toward justifying all of the near (and worse) misses that happened along the way to that mythical perfect performance.

Add to this the fact that opera is very, very expensive. In fact, it's invariably a losing proposition, and it always has been. In its early days, it relied entirely on aristocratic subsidies for its existence. A private opera company was in many ways the ultimate luxury and example of conspicuous consumption. After all, it had no purpose other than entertainment, and in the process to serve as a tribute to the taste and culture of the reigning monarch or patron.

Now those subsidies come from the government, the wealthy, and/or from preferential tax treatment. For brief periods in its history opera may have been popular enough to survive on its own for a few years, but these oases in what is otherwise a desert of financial ruin remain exceptions to the general rule. The fact that Handel was able to earn a living from opera, however precarious it sometimes was, and later from his oratorios, stands as one of the greatest triumphs of human stamina and determination in the history of the arts. Even he, however, received a supplemental annual allowance directly from the Crown. He couldn't readily have survived without it.

Opera, then, is paradoxical. On the one hand, it is uniquely collaborative, requiring the cooperation of a vast number of musical and nonmusical artists, all working toward a shared goal. At the same time, however, it demands the presence of individual star voices. Handel advertised his operas on two fronts: for their top-quality casts, and on the basis of their innovative staging and lavish costumes. Some audience members undoubtedly came primarily for the visual element, to see the spectacle. What kept them coming back, however, was the singing, and this needs to be understood as an element distinct from the absolute quality of the composition. Whether good music or bad, the performance *had* to be fabulous.

The singing, you see, offered the aural equivalent to the spectacle, a feast for the ear to match or even exceed that for the eye, and spectacular it was. However, if opera ultimately remains a singer's medium, its written history more often has been shaped by scholars to read as an ongoing conflict between the prerogatives of the performers versus those of the composers and librettists. It makes for a good story, with the heroic "reformers," usually Germans, such as Gluck and Wagner, redeeming music from the depredations of vulgar singers and composers willing to work within the debased, invariably Italian, status quo. It is also bunk. Don't get me wrong: Gluck and Wagner were both great reformers and great composers, but if they hadn't written rewarding roles for their singers, we would not be discussing them now.

Handel's operas, and baroque *opera seria* more generally, fit into my construct in their own unique way. It is too simplistic to portray the revival of these works as a triumph of modern scholarship in the area of "applied musicology"; that is, the recovery of historically informed performance practices and techniques. This may be how the history is being written. For sure, the contributions of the scholarly community to the performance of baroque music have had tremendous significance, and have added immeasurably to our musical enjoyment. There is no question about that, but it's still not the whole story, nor even necessarily the most crucial element.

It is true that the Handel opera revival over the course of the twentieth century grew out of the gradual recovery and interest in baroque music more generally, including such composers as Bach and Vivaldi, as well as the training of musicians able to interpret the music is a reasonably convincing way. I won't say *authentic*, because the better word would be *proprietary*. Modern performers combine technical mastery of certain elements of baroque style—of such practices as ornamentation and improvisation—with a unique sound that strikes our ears as idiomatic to the work at hand. It doesn't have to be authentic as much as it is special.

However, none of these archaeological efforts, admirable as they are, would have been nearly as effective without the realization that baroque opera contains numerous roles full of star potential; and that discovery rightly belongs, not to the scholarly community, but to singers working to establish themselves in the traditional way—by finding music that they could make their own. I am thinking of three artists in particular, none of whom were baroque specialists as we understand that term now: Joan Sutherland, Beverly Sills, and somewhat later, Marilyn Horne. Had they not appeared in tandem with the ongoing baroque revival, from the late 1950s through the 1980s, the much-vaunted rediscovery of Handel's operas that began in Göttingen, Germany, in the 1920s might well have remained an event of merely academic interest. Timing is everything.

The great role most significantly associated with Sutherland, who sang Handel throughout her career, was Alcina, the sorceress undone by the power of love in the eponymous opera. She brought the role to La Fenice opera house in Venice in 1960, and made her United States debut with it in Dallas that same year. Covent Garden staged the work for her in 1962, and she recorded the complete opera, or her version of it, for Decca. The part not only earned tremendous acclaim for the most exciting new singer on the international scene since Maria Callas, it afforded her a proprietary repertoire in music long thought to be not just obsolete, but virtually unsingable. Thanks to Sutherland, a Handel opera suddenly became internationally viable as a box office attraction—provided she was around to sing it, of course.

The next milestone in the Handel opera revival occurred in 1966, when Beverly Sills became an international celebrity for her appearance as Cleopatra in the New York City Opera's production of *Giulio Cesare*, a role she also recorded. As with Sutherland, recordings played a major part in spreading the word about both the singer and the work. Scholars love to turn up their nose at this production, and certainly it is inauthentic by modern standards in just about every way that's possible. The title role went, not to a woman or male falsettist, but to Norman Treigle, a bass-baritone better known for his performances of Mussorgsky's Boris Godunov and Boito's Mefistofele. Various cuts and rearrangements of the score were guaranteed to drive subsequent purists crazy.

And yet, there is one sense in which the production was more "authentic" than what we view as such today: the opera was built up around the cast, exactly as Handel himself did it. It gave the singers an opportunity to shine, and made Sills's career. She had been hanging out as a "house soprano" for years until she got her lungs on Cleopatra. It is easy to find opera lovers who insist to this day that, in its combination of technical virtuosity allied to emotional truth, there has never been a more gripping and complete portrayal than hers. No one goes to hear an opera to experience scholarly correctness; they go to hear great singing.

Last, but certainly not least, there is Marilyn Horne, a one-woman revival if ever there was one. Horne's voice stands among the most remarkable of the twentieth century. Technically she was a mezzo-soprano, but her range was huge and perfectly even, from a baritonal chest register to a bright, firm soprano top. She could spit out more notes per second than just about anyone alive, always with near supernatural accuracy of pitch and rhythm. Her diction was impeccable. She was the closest we will probably ever get to the sound of a Handelian castrato, at least as those voices were described by those who actually heard them.

Accordingly, although well known as an impressive Handel singer in recital and on recordings from early in her career, when she finally took

on complete operas Horne sang the guys: Orlando and Rinaldo specifically, both of whom she recorded live. Her performance of Rinaldo at
the Metropolitan Opera in 1984 marked the first time that a Handel
opera had ever been staged there.

All of Handel's operas require star castrato singers, although it's
easy to make too much of this. Female artists who specialized in taking
male roles also were in great demand, and many parts were written for
them expressly. As with baroque orchestration, the *register* of the voice,
whether it was high, and thus "on top," or low, was more important than
the sex of the singer. When Handel couldn't find a castrato who was
suitable, he employed a woman—almost never a countertenor (known
at the time as "falsettists," among other things), such as we use today
in the name of "authenticity." For example in *Ariodante*, the alto role of
Polinesso, Duke of Albany, may have been written for a female singer
because Handel lacked a second castrato in his pool of artists, but this
was by no means a second-best option.

The reason for his preference is simple: castratos did not sing with
that unsupported falsetto tone so characteristic of the countertenor
voice. They employed their natural (if you'll pardon the term) range,
which for many just happened to be that of a mezzo-soprano, such as
Marilyn Horne. Her timbre, accordingly, is more "masculine," or at all
events more convincingly heroic, than just about any of the men who
until very recently sang the same parts in modern productions; and
make no mistake, some of them are astoundingly fine artists with very
beautiful voices. Historically correct, though? No.

Horne's achievement cannot be overestimated, even if she was better
known as a Rossini and *bel canto* specialist. There have always been
so-called trouser roles in opera—lots of them, actually—women who
sing the parts of young men. The most famous is probably Cherubino
in Mozart's *The Marriage of Figaro*. Richard Strauss loved the concept
too: think of Octavian in *Der Rosenkavalier*, or The Composer in *Ariadne
auf Naxos*, but these are more often not the star attractions. The warrior Arsace in Rossini's *Semiramide*, on the other hand, is a lead role,
and it, too, became a Horne specialty (opposite Joan Sutherland as the
title character).

Marilyn Horne proved that a woman singing heroic male parts could fill an opera house, and thus, that one of the stranger theatrical conventions of Handel's day presented no barrier to enjoyment. That willful suspension of disbelief mentioned in the last chapter could be stretched just a tad further without fear. Why? I'll say it again: *Because all opera is about great singing*, however it gets there. This same fact also explains the success of today's best countertenors, artists such as David Daniels, Bejun Mehta, Max Emanuel Cencic, Andreas Scholl, and Philippe Jaroussky, who are interpreting the heroic castrato roles in a progressively more convincing style.

The success of Sutherland, Sills, and Horne encouraged younger singers to take up the baroque repertoire. Those three pioneers showed that it could be done, and that you could potentially make a living doing it, but none of them staked their careers on Handel alone. All three preferred to focus on later music, the romantic bel canto repertoire of the early nineteenth century especially. Handel, and baroque music more generally from about the 1970s, was rapidly becoming the province of early music specialists. Conservatories accordingly began churning out superbly trained "baroque" singers by the boatload.

At the same time, in the 1970s through the 1990s, record labels were desperate for new repertoire, or marketable reasons to issue new versions of established classics. Arts organizations, despite their incessant protests to the contrary, were awash in funds and needed to justify their subsidies and tax breaks by staking out proprietary, niche repertoire. Baroque *opera seria* provided a blank slate on which avant-garde theatrical producers could inflict their "vision" on a venerable masterpiece, for good or ill, supposedly making it more "relevant" for modern audiences.

Handel was the perfect composer to benefit from the above scenario: a certified classic who wrote three and a half *dozen* almost totally neglected operas. Musicologists assisted in publishing clean critical editions, coaching performers in historical performance practice, and in general providing a framework that gave artists new and useful paradigms on which to base their musical interpretations. In other words, they explained how it was possible to respect the composer's original text and still put on a good show.

For a while, the two main currents of Handel opera performance—the "historically informed" and the more traditional, big theater productions—proceeded in parallel. At the present time, however, many of the discoveries advanced by the historically minded school as "authentic" have been absorbed by today's established ensembles and singers. The two currents have converged. Early music conductors routinely appear on the podiums of major symphony orchestras and opera houses. Handel's theatrical output has become mainstream once again. The spectacle that is baroque opera is back in business.

Ariodante: Handel's Operatic Paradigm

The list at the head of this chapter consists of forty-two operas: all that survive more or less intact. They have been exhaustively studied by the late Winton Dean in his two-volume masterpiece, *Handel's Operas*, and if you're truly hard-core I can recommend it with enthusiasm. It's a great read. The size of Handel's operatic output makes it impossible to discuss with anything like Dean's attention to detail, especially in the single chapter of a general survey of the composer. Also, while most of the operas have now been recorded, the less familiar ones may only have appeared once, and then not always in the most persuasive performances. Still, it goes without saying that "unfamiliar" does not mean "bad" or "uninteresting," and you certainly can collect them at your leisure if you so choose.

Since our focus is on strategies for listening, I decided to limit the remaining discussion first, to a close look at a single opera as a paradigm for the medium, and then to describe briefly the dozen operas generally viewed as among the greatest, as well as the most frequently recorded. This increases the likelihood that you will actually have the opportunity to hear them. At the end of this chapter I will also mention some of the best aria collections and recital discs—a perfectly legitimate and often very enjoyable way to get to know the larger works, as well as the major artists who perform them.

I want to begin, then, by taking a close look at one of Handel's best and most approachable operas, *Ariodante*, so as to make some

generalizations about *opera seria*, and also to focus your attention on
those elements that could be adjusted or personalized from one work
to the next. Even though no two Handel operas are exactly alike, the
medium forces certain constraints on every composer. Just consider
the implications of the fact that it was often expected that a new opera
would be written in a matter of, say, six to eight weeks (or less), and that
it be cast, rehearsed, and premiered just a few days after completion.

The singers, in particular, had to learn their roles very quickly,
and to make their task easier they had to know what to expect. For
example, a da capo aria in ABA form is convenient because the singer
only needs to learn "A" and "B." The reprise of "A" requires improvised
ornamentation, which could either be planned in advance or made
up on the spot. The form showcases the singer's virtuosity, taste, and
intelligence, and offers a good bit of solo time in front of the audience.
In this way conventions are born, and *opera seria* had a bunch of them
that composers ignored at their peril. Any significant deviation from the
norm had to be special, usually—if the composer was smart—reserved
for moments of high drama. Knowing just when to foil expectations is
one of those qualities that distinguishes Handel's genius as a composer
for the theater.

In general, then, there is less formal variety in the operas than you
will find in the oratorios. The main unit of expression is the da capo
aria, either preceded or followed by a keyboard-accompanied secco
("dry") recitative containing dialogue to move the plot along. One
of Handel's constraints turns out to be a mercy for modern English-
speaking listeners. Because his audience did not speak Italian and
likely had no appreciation of Italian poetry, he took pains to reduce the
amount of secco recitative to a bare minimum. This means less "talk,"
more music, and a swifter development of the action.

At moments of extreme tension the strings can accompany recitative, a process previously mentioned and called "accompagnato." A
duet, a trio, a chorus, or an instrumental interlude might interrupt
the standard, long chain of solo arias now and then, but always infre-
quently. You might think that all of this sounds terribly formulaic, and
it certainly can be with an uninspired composer, but as always with
such things the devil is in the details. Consider the usual da capo aria:

ABA, and imagine what opportunities this offers someone with a little bit of imagination.

First, call it what you will, at the end of the day an "aria" is just a song, and we all know what those are. Handel wrote thousands of them over his career, and not just for operas. There are even a goodly number of individual, stand-alone songs, and if you're curious you can buy a delightful disc of them—titled *The Occasional Songs*—featuring Emma Kirkby, on the Somm label. The da capo aria, then, is merely a specific kind of song out of which composers in Handel's day constructed operas and other large vocal works.

One major advantage of this form lies in the potential contrasts between the "A" and "B" sections: fast or slow, loud or soft, major or minor, development of existing material or something entirely new, as well as changes in scoring. Second, as noted, the repeat of "A" will be ornamented, but this can mean anything from the additional of a few trills, turns, or other doodads, to an entirely revamped vocal melody from start to finish. In general, slow and lyrical music will only be embellished minimally, but in the quick stuff, full of vocal fireworks, the sky is the limit. You can hear this principle at work very clearly in the arias included on the sample CD. Even the length can vary hugely. Handel's da capo forms can last anywhere from less than thirty seconds to about fifteen minutes.

Now, take a moment to consider just the "A" section. The standard form begins with an orchestral tune, or ritornello, followed by a vocal entry singing the first couple of lines of text. The ritornello then returns, usually in modified or abridged form, leading to a second vocal episode repeating the same words in various ways. There is no practical rule that determines the relationship between the ritornello and the vocal melody. They can be identical, merely similar in some details, or completely different. Some arias will reserve the ritornello until the end of the "A" section and begin with the voice right away, or after just a few bars.

Also, not all da capo arias are really da capo. The composer can short-circuit the repeat by going directly to the vocal entrance and omitting the ritornello, or pick up the music someplace in the middle. This type of aria is called *dal segno*, or "from the sign" that tells the performers where the repeat actually begins. If the ritornello is very long, abbreviating or omitting it the second time around tightens up the form and speeds up the sequence of musical events. Handel, as we will see, often preferred this kind of structure.

Finally, there is the type of aria that Winton Dean called a cavatina, after the later Italian term for a short, lyrical, usually slow number without any large sectional repeats at all. "Ombra mai fu" is a cavatina. Handel called it an arioso. As in this most famous example from the opening scene of *Serse*, cavatinas come in handy when introducing new characters or giving expression to simple, plaintive feelings without holding up the action for too long. Even here, the relationship between vocal and instrumental themes can vary considerably.

There is a tremendous amount of freedom and variety built into this very simple aria form. That is the point really: the simplicity offers composers a blank slate capable of the widest variety of expression, while at the same time providing singers with ease of memorization, a certain standard vocabulary of affect, and plenty of crowd-pleasing moments. And as with all such schematic forms, small changes can have surprisingly large impacts if only because it's so easy play with the listener's expectations.

With this in mind, let us now have a look at an outline of Handel's *Ariodante*. I also trace the plot, note a few scene changes where they seem relevant, and offer some brief commentary on the individual numbers.[8]

Ariodante Outline

Cast—1735 and 1736 revision

Ariodante: a knight-prince, engaged to Ginevra (soprano castrato)

Ginevra: a Scottish princess, engaged to Ariodante (soprano)

King (bass): Ginevra's father, king of Scotland

Lurcanio (tenor): Ariodante's brother, in love with Dalinda

Polinesso (alto—bass in 1736 revival): Duke of Albany, the villain

Dalinda (soprano—alto in 1736 revival): Polinesso's wannabe girlfriend
    and attendant to Ginevra

Odoardo (tenor—bass in 1736 revival): a courtier

Orchestra (as listed in the score): 2 recorders, 2 flutes, 2 oboes, bas-
    soon, 2 horns, 2 trumpets, strings (with violins in up to 3 parts),
    continuo (cello, bass, bassoon, lute(s), harpsichord)
Stage Band (in final scene): 2 oboes and bassoon

Orchestra in the recommended Minkowski recording (one practical
    realization of the above): 2 flutes/recorders, 4 oboes, 3 bassoons, 2
    horns/trumpets, 16 violins, 4 violas, 5 cellos (one for the continuo),
    3 basses (one for the continuo), harpsichord, theorbo (lute), baroque
    guitar
Stage band drawn from the above group

Key to Aria Types

cavatina: (an aria with an "A" section only; Handel often called it
    "arioso")
dc: da capo (ABA: go back to the beginning and repeat "A" with
    ornaments)
ds: dal segno (ABA: go back to the sign and repeat from there with
    ornaments)

Note on scoring: where strings and continuo are not mentioned their
presence is assumed.

Music (as per 1735 original version)
Overture [oboes]
Gavotte [oboes, bassoon]

First Act
Scene 1 (a room in the palace)
1. Aria (Cavatina): "Vezzi, lusinghe" (Ginevra) [violins in 3 parts]
Recitative (Dalinda, Ginevra)

*In this graceful arioso opening number Ginevra, at her dressing table,
sings of her love and hopes that Ariodante will find her attractive. She and
Dalinda make small talk.*

Scene 2
Recitative (Polinesso, Ginevra)
2. Aria (dc): "Orrida agli occhi miei" (Ginevra) [strings]

Polinesso enters and declares his love. Ginevra rebuffs him in the strongest possible language, saying that the sight of him disgusts her. This short, lively da capo aria appropriately starts with the voice, and only concludes with the ritornello. It ends with Handel's typical "quick" gesture, a falling "snap" of an octave.

Scene 3
Recitative (Polinesso, Dalinda)
3. Aria (dc): "Apri le luci" (Dalinda) [strings]

Dalinda tells Polinesso that his love of Ginevra is futile, and (in the aria) that he should open his eyes to the possibility that he may be loved by others (like herself, for example). The orchestral introduction is only a couple of bars long.

Scene 4
Recitative (Polinesso)
4. Aria (ds): "Coperta la frode" (Polinesso) [oboes]

This aria is a soliloquy: Polinesso muses that Dalinda's love for him will, through treachery, keep Ariodante from the crown. Again, the introduction is very short, and though technically a dal segno and not a da capo, it is in fact indistinguishable in form from Dalinda's previous aria. Notice that all of these initial arias have been short and brisk, setting the action in motion with no delay.

Scene 5
5. Aria (Cavatina): "Qui d'amor nel suo linguaggio" (Ariodante) [oboes]
Recitative (Ariodante, Ginevra)
6. Duet (Continuous, Segue Recitative): "Prendi da questa mano" (Ginevra, Ariodante) [strings]

The first truly slow music in the opera, this cavatina, recitative, and duet function as a single unit, and the continuity is only reinforced when the duet flows into the ensuing recitative with the entrance of the king. The mood is that of an idyllic pastoral.

Scene 6
Recitative (King, Ginevra, Ariodante)
7. Aria (ds): "Volate, amori" (Ginevra) [oboes]

The king gives his blessing to Ariodante and Ginevra's union, and Ginevra sings a jig of pure happiness, with lots of brilliant coloratura. Note the unexpected initial entry of the voice, seemingly in midritornello. The ending is equally unexpected.

Scene 7
Recitative (King, Odoardo)
8. Aria (ds): "Voli colla sua tromba" (King) [oboes, horns]

The king tells Odoardo to get ready to announce the big news, and the horns do just that in his ensuing hefty and celebratory aria.

Scene 8
Recitative (Ariodante)
9. Aria (ds): "Con l'ali di costanza" (Ariodante) [strings]

Now it's Ariodante's turn to sing of his happiness in the most virtuosic aria yet. Carestini, the castrato who sang the first Ariodante, evidently had an absolutely sensational technique. Note the abbreviated ritornello on the repeat, a typical use of the dal segno indication. This ritornello also uses Handel's quick ending of a descending octave.

Scene 9
Recitative (Polinesso, Dalinda)
10. Aria (ds): "Spero per voi, sì, sì" (Polinesso) [strings]

The plot thickens: Polinesso says that if Dalinda dresses up as Ginevra and lets him in to her chamber that evening, he will return Dalinda's love. Polinesso's initial, sexy "Spero" ("I hope") seems to promise love, but the continuation suggests otherwise. The repeat, though, lays on the insincerity even thicker.

Scene 10
Recitative (Lurcanio, Dalinda)
11. Aria (ds): "Del mio sol vezzosi rai" (Lurcanio) [oboes]

*Lurcanio declares his love to Dalinda. She rejects him kindly, but he sings
a desperate love aria whose syncopated rhythms wonderfully underscore his
confusion and instability.*

Scene 11
Recitative (Dalinda)
12. Aria (ds): "Il primo ardor" (Dalinda) [oboes]

*Alone, Dalinda insists with spirit that her devotion to Polinesso will never
weaken.*

Scene 12 (a delightful valley [presumably near the palace])
*The remainder of the act is essentially a celebration of the forthcoming
union of Ariodante and Ginevra, complete with visual spectacle in the form
of a pastoral ballet. Its purpose is entertainment, plain and simple.*

Recitative (Ariodante)

Scene 13
Recitative (Ginevra, Ariodante)
13. Sinfonia [oboes, bassoon, horns]
14. Duet e Chorus: "Se rinasce nel mio cor" (Ginevra, Ariodante,
    Chorus) [oboes, bassoon, horns]
    Ballet of nymphs, shepherds and shepherdesses
15. Ballo [oboes, bassoon, horns]
16. Musette I [flute]
17. Musette II [flute]
18. No marking [2 recorders]
17. Chorus and Solos: "Sì, godete al vostro amor" (Chorus, Ginevra,
    Ariodante) [oboes, bassoon, horns]

First intermission: time to get up, stretch, run to the lobby, and buy
an overpriced orangeade. This first act contains mostly quick, or at all
events forceful music, and it admirably sets up the action to follow. Out
of eleven arias, only two follow strict da capo form, even though most

still retain that typical ABA shape. Don't make yourself crazy trying to figure out where the "segno" will be in the others. The point is that, contrary to stereotype, the plot moves along with impressive speed and the arias—even the longer ones—do nothing to get in the way.

Second Act

Scene 1 (a moonlit garden in a ruin with a secret door leading to Ginevra's apartment in the palace)
20. Sinfonia [strings]
Recitative (Polinesso)

The opening sinfonia beautifully conjures up a moonlit night—the tune is in the bass, with soft string chords above. Polinesso awaits Ariodante so that he can set his plan in motion with Dalinda dressed as Ginevra.

Scene 2
Recitative (Polinesso, Ariodante, Lurcanio)
21. Aria (ds): "Tu, preparati a morire" (Ariodante) [strings]
Recitative (Polinesso, Dalina, Lurcanio, Ariodante)
22. Aria (ds): "Tu vivi" (Lurcanio) [violins]

A big scene with two arias in which just about everyone participates. Ariodante appears and tells Polinesso he's to be married to Ginevra. "That's strange," Polinesso replies, "since she's my lover. If you don't believe me, just wait a minute and you'll see." Ariodante hides himself, but not before telling Polinesso in the scene's first aria that if he is lying, he's toast. The "A" section is full of bluster; the very long "B" section in slower tempo speaks of Ariodante's despair if Ginevra has deceived him.

Dalinda appears as Ginevra, and Polinesso goes inside with her. Ariodante tries to kill himself, but Lurcanio, who has been conveniently spying on everyone, appears and takes Ariodante's sword, telling him that a faithless woman isn't worth dying for. Here's another aria with Handel's patented quick ending.

Scene 3
Recitative (Ariodante)
23. Aria (ds): "Scherza, infida" (Ariodante) [muted strings, bassoon]

Ariodante's recitative is only about fifteen seconds long. "I live, but have not even a sword," he says in disgust. The aria that follows is one of Handel's greatest, and arguably the expressive highpoint of the opera. Ariodante laments his betrayal—to the creepy accompaniment of muted strings and bassoon—and vows to return from beyond the grave to haunt the deceitful Ginevra forever. In this dal segno aria, which is quite long, Handel drops the ritornello entirely for the repeat of the "A" section, starting immediately with Ariodante's entrance.

Scene 4

Recitative (Polinesso, Dalinda)
24. Aria (Cavatina): "Se tanto piace al cor" (Dalinda) [strings]

Polinesso tells Dalinda that they have succeeded, and that she has earned his love. She sings the gentle siciliano aria on the accompanying disc, which we explore in greater detail in chapter 7.

Scene 5

Recitative (Polinesso)
25. Aria (ds): "Se l'inganno sortisce felice" (Polinesso) [strings]

Every villain has a scene where he gloats, and here Shakespeare's Iago, from Othello, *stands especially close behind. "Honesty gets you nowhere," Polinesso observes. This aria serves the additional purpose of injecting a good dose of energy into the proceedings after the previous two slow and reflective pieces. Note, though, all three arias remain in minor keys. The mood is consistently dark, and it's about to get darker.*

Scene 6

Recitative (King, Odoardo)
26a. Aria (ds): "Invida sorte avara" (King) [violins]
or
26b. Aria (dc): "Più contento e più felice" (King) [violins]

The king is about to declare Ariodante as his heir when Odoardo runs in and announces that, for reasons unknown, Ariodante has thrown himself into the sea and died. Shocked, the king sings either aria 26a, which Handel originally wrote, or 26b, which was actually sung at the premiere. The first is another dark siciliano similar to Dalinda's, in which he describes his abject misery at the news; 26b is a more philosophical and chipper observation on how quickly happiness can turn to sorrow. Most performances prefer 26a because it's much sadder, but that may have been precisely the reason Handel decided to lighten the mood at this point.

Scene 7
27. Aria (ds): "Mi palpita il core" (Genevra) [oboes]
Recitative (Dalinda, King, Ginevra)

Genevra, alone, feels a dark sense of foreboding. The king enters and tells her the terrible news. She faints.

Scene 8
Recitative (Lurcanio, King)
28. Aria (ds): "Il tuo sangue" (Lurcanio) [strings]

Lurcanio comes to the king demanding justice; he blames Ginevra for his brother's death and will duel with anyone who chooses to defend her (being a loose woman was a capital offence in medieval Scotland, as everyone knows). He tells the king, in a very vigorous aria (with Handel's quick ending), that he must choose between being a monarch and being a father.

Scene 9
Recitative (Odoardo, Dalinda, Ginevra, King)

Ginevera and Dalinda then approach the king; he calls his daughter a slut and walks out.

Scene 10
29. Accompagnato (Accompanied Recitative): A me impudica? (Ginevra, Dalinda) [strings]
30. Aria (ds): "Il mio crudel martoro" (Ginevra) [violins]

Slut shaming is always a big moment in opera of every period, and so we get a passionate and dynamic accompanied recitative between Ginevra and Dalinda. Ginevra is bewildered; Dalinda, ingenuous. Ginevera's aria, in which she asks for death, is her answer to Ariodante's "Scherza infida"—her emotional nadir. You may notice that Handel points up the similarity by quoting the accompanying, sobbing rhythmic figure from the previous aria. The two lovers are now united in sorrow.

Really Original Version of Second Act Finale
31a. Entrée des Songes agréables (ballet) [strings]
31b. Entrée des Songes funestes (ballet) [strings]
31c. Entrée des Songes agréables effrayés (ballet) [strings]
31d. Le combat des Songes funestes et agréables (ballet) [strings]
32a. Accompagnato: "Che vidi?" (Ginevra) [strings]

Having retired to sleep, Ginevra has a vision of a battle between pleasant and evil dreams. The music illustrates the action perfectly: first the pleasant dreams, then the evil dreams, then the pleasant dreams return, frightened, and the two groups do battle. Ginevra awakens in confusion, remarking that she finds no peace even in sleep. And so the act ends very dramatically with a brief accompanied recitative. This is the version invariably staged and recorded. The alternative used at the first performance is much tamer. Handel later moved the original dances to his next opera, Alcina, *so if you really like them you get to hear them twice.*

Version of Second Act Finale from First Performance
31. Entrée de'Mori (ballet) [strings]
32. Rondeau (ballet) [oboes]

Second Intermission: Only one true da capo aria in this act (out of nine). The first act was very high voltage, but had little plot. The musical energy alone carries the audience along. This act, in contrast, forms a complete contrast. There is a great deal of plot, but even more tension and atmosphere, most of it in very dark, intense arias featuring slow tempos and minor keys. Because of this, the loud eruptions, such as Polinesso's and Lurcanio's arias, as well as the concluding accompanied recitatives and ballet, are all the more vivid. No matter which version is used, the ending leaves us in high suspense.

Third Act

Scene 1 (a forest)

33. Aria (Cavatina): "Numi! Lasciarmi vivere" (Ariodante) [strings]

Recitative (Dalinda, Ariodante)

34. Aria (ds): "Cieca notte" (Ariodante) [strings]

The first scene includes two arias. In the first, a cavatina, Ariodante (disguised) asks the gods why they let him live if only to suffer. Enter Dalinda, pursued by two assassins hired by Polinesso to keep her permanently quiet. Ariodante drives them off; they recognize each other, and Dalinda, understandably pissed, spills the beans on Polinesso. Ariodante sings of how easily he has been deceived.

Scene 2

Recitative (Dalinda)

35. Aria (ds): "Neghittosi, or voi che fatte?" (Dalinda) [violins]

Dalinda, now alone, sings the obligatory (but always flashy and fun) Vengeance Aria. This is a standard type, as with love songs, laments, heroic calls to battle, and simile arias involving boats sailing safely into port, snakes strangling their prey, lions pouncing, and other stereotypical imagery. In this classic example, Dalinda calls on heaven to strike Polinesso with lightening, tear him from limb to limb, punish him for all eternity, and there's also something about rocks and temples that makes no sense at all, but really, does it matter? Note that the tonality has remained mostly in the minor, but that is about to change.

Scene 3

Recitative (Odoardo, King, Polinesso)

36. Aria (ds): "Dover, giustizia, amor" (Polinesso) [oboes]

The king orders that the lists be readied for Ginevera's judgment by battle. Polinesso, with unseemly arrogance, sings in a zippy and gloating aria that he will be her defender (hoping to kill Lurcanio and thus win Ginevera for himself).

Scene 4
Recitative (King)

The king asks to see Ginevera.

Scene 5
Recitative (King, Ginevra)
37. Aria (ds): "Io to bacio" (Ginevra) [strings]
Recitative (King, Ginevra)
38. Aria (ds): "Al sen ti stringo" (King) [flutes]

Ginevera protests her innocence and expresses her love for her father despite her unjust treatment. She kisses his hand, singing an exquisite and very lightly accompanied aria full of hesitation and sadness. He tells her that Polinesso has agreed to defend her honor. She tries to refuse the offer, but the king says he wishes it. He bids her farewell in a touching siciliano, with flutes joining the strings to add a touch of extra warmth to t he sound.

Scene 6
Recitative (Ginevra)
39. Aria (Cavatina, attacca Sinfonia): "Sì, morrò" (Ginevra) [solo violin, solo cello, violins in 3 parts]
40. Sinfonia [oboes, trumpet]

In this wonderful scene, Ginevra begins with what seems like another lament, but suddenly wakes up and rages against the insult to her honor that has been inflicted on her. She has a backbone, it seems. This brief cavatina runs directly into the sinfonia, introducing . . .

Scene 7
Recitative (Lurcanio, Polinesso, Odoardo, King)

The battle between Lurcanio and Polinesso: Lurcanio wins, Polinesso is taken off to die, and the king rises from his throne and says that he will now defend his daughter's honor. Suddenly . . .

Scene 8
Recitative (Ariodante, King, Lurcanio)

Ariodante appears to defend Ginevra. He raises his visor, shocking everyone that he's still alive, and agrees to tell all if the king will pardon Dalinda for a slight (ahem) misdeed.

Scene 9
Recitative (King, Dalinda, Odoardo)
41. Aria (ds): "Dopo notte, atra e funesta" (Ariodante) [violins in 3 parts]

Odoardo reports that Polinesso confessed his treachery with his dying breath. The king pardons Dalinda, and Ariodante sings a showstopper of an aria of "the dark night has passed" variety. Because this is baroque opera, however, the "B" section also just has to refer to a ship sailing safely into port after a storm (We've heard that one a few times before, right?). This is one of those operatic moments where everyone else just stands there and listens, as does the audience, to some really spectacular singing.

Scene 10
Recitative (Lurcanio, Dalinda)
42. Duet (continuous): "Dite spera, e son contento" (Lurcanio, Dalinda) [violins]

Lurcanio and Dalinda kiss and make up.

Scene 11
Recitative (Ginevra)
43. Arioso and Sinfonia: "Manca, oh Dei!" (Ginevra) [strings, then oboes and horns]

Meanwhile, Ginevra, imprisoned in her room, has no idea what has been going on. She is still praying for death when, happily, her elegiac but brief cavatina is interrupted after just a few bars by joyous music. This is similar to what happened in her previous cavatina, but in keeping with the urgency of the drama the interruptions come in sooner, making Ginevera's part progressively shorter. It's sort of a musical parallel to her approaching rescue and vindication.

Scene 12
Sinfonia (as previous)

Recitative (King, Ariodante, Dalinda, Lurcanio, Ginevra)

44. Duet (continuous): "Bramo aver mille vite" (Ariodante, Ginevra) [strings]

All of the above enter and tell Ginevra, well, you know what they tell her. She and Ariodante sing a joyful duet expressing their happiness, and the king declares a festival of music and dancing to celebrate the happy outcome.

Final Scene

45. Chorus: "Ognuno acclami" [stage band, trumpets]
46. Gavotte (ballet) [stage band]
47. Rondeau (ballet) [stage band]
48. No marking (ballet) [oboes]
49. Chorus: "Sa trionfar ognor" [stage band, horns]

End of the opera.

As you can see, there are no da capo arias in the third act. They are all dal segnos or cavatinas. Also, similar to the first act, we find two duets close to the end, a nice parallel and a good way to help build to the final climax by increasing the variety of musical incident. In act 3 especially, the "finale" really begins in scene 6, with Ginevra's cavatina "Sì, morrò." From that point on the music is effectively continuous. Even though there is still a good bit of explanatory secco recitative, the sequence of events and revelations is so swift that it just sweeps you along right through to the end.

The lesson, then, is that the old saw holding that "recitative = plot dialogue," while "arias = frozen moments of emotional expression" is way too simplistic. There are arias the move the action along, and some that slow it down, just as recitative (irrespective of what it says) can pique the listener's interest in the story, or kill an act's building momentum entirely. It's all a question of how the composer groups and contrasts the individual numbers and sections. *Ariodante*, and Handel's operas generally, almost never come across as a random assortments of stop and go moments. They are all "go."

There are aspects of *Ariodante* that are very typical of Handel's operas, and some that are unique to this particular work. General features include:

1. The three-act structure. All of Handel's operas have three acts with the single exception of *Teseo*. That work is based on a five-act French model, and French baroque opera is a world unto itself. *Teseo*, incidentally, features the famous character of the sorceress Medea (she tries to poison him in this opera) who earned several operas to herself, including the famous work by Luigi Cherubini that Maria Callas made iconic.

2. The division into numbered scenes depends on who is on stage and means little else. In general, the arrival or departure of a character indicates a new scene. This may or may not affect the musical flow.

3. It was a very strong convention in baroque opera that the singer exits the stage after each aria. This offered the opportunity to receive and acknowledge applause from the audience. It may be that Handel discarded the original ballet at the end of act 2 because it emerged out of Ginevra's aria, leaving her on stage pretending to be asleep. Even though she ends the act by herself, it would certainly have taken some convincing to get a singer to agree to do it that way. Handel also sometimes violates this rule in his cavatinas; they are not "major" arias and so the character can remain to participate in the following recitative.

4. The "single affect rule" states that an aria or movement should only express a single emotion, or affect. It was a widely held point of aesthetics, but it's probably safe to say that few composers felt very strongly bound by it. The very nature of an ABA form suggests at least two contrasting ideas or feelings. Ginevra's "Sì, morrò" contains two distinct musical and expressive ideas within a single formal unit. In other words, this is one of those "rules" that asks to be kept in mind so as to enjoy the many different ways in which it *isn't* followed.

5. Length: each act plays for about an hour, making the total running time of the opera about three hours. This is typical. Some Handel operas are a bit longer (*Giulio Cesare*, for example), and many are

shorter, but two and a half to three hours is the norm—and this standard carries over into the oratorios too.

6. Number of individual items. Ariodante contains forty-nine specific pieces, including all of the arias, duets, choruses, accompagnatos, and ballet movements, but excluding secco recitative. Round it off to about fifty, and you have a good sense of what to expect in a Handel opera or oratorio generally.

Features unique to *Ariodante*, or to Handel particularly, include:

1. The ballet episodes. French baroque opera is equal parts singing and dancing, but ballet in Italian opera that is really part of the action, as opposed to an independent work, is relatively rare. For a few years, Handel had a French ballet company at his disposal led by the (for the day) avant-garde dancer Marie Sallé. He made full use of her troupe while he could, until it was banished from England for being too sexy and, well, French.

2. A tenor. Handel was one of the first composers to exploit the tenor voice, most tellingly in the character of Bajazet in *Tamerlano*. Lurcanio is another example. In this case John Beard, a tenor who for decades created roles in all of Handel's major oratorios, sang the part. His presence offered an alternative to the general reliance on castratos, providing a new type of male lead.

3. That original, second act ending. It is indicative of just how strong the "aria-exit to applause" convention was that Handel concluded no other act in any other opera, according to Winton Dean, with an accompanied recitative.

4. *Ariodante* belongs to a cluster of three great operas all based on Ludovico Ariosto's epic poem *Orlando furioso*. The others are *Orlando* and *Alcina*.

5. The late-classical composer Simon Mayr set the same story as *Ariodante* in 1801, calling it *Ginevra di Scozia* (1801). Both operas are based on an earlier libretto by Antonio Salvi (in turn developed from Ariosto). Mayr's opera has been recorded for Opera Rara, and is worth a listen.

6. Use of different aria types. *Ariodante*, as we saw, contains an unusually low number of strict da capo arias, even for Handel. This is

neither good nor bad in an absolute sense, but it tells us something about the kind of swift dramatic pacing that Handel felt the story demanded.

To get the most out of baroque opera, as the above suggests, a key strategy is to have a sense of what the conventions are so you can enjoy listening to a great composer both observe and ignore them. The ones that really matter are neither numerous nor complicated. If you have read this far then you know everything that you need to. Most of the other "rules" are just common sense: things like giving each singer enough to do while organizing each act in logical sequence. However limiting the requirement to accommodate the demands of singers may have been, baroque composers still wrote masterpieces of musical drama, and the demands of the artists did not necessarily conflict with theatrical imperatives all of the time. Certainly Handel didn't think so.

A Dozen Great Handel Operas (excluding *Ariodante*)

Here are another dozen works that you will find worth investigating. Each has elements, easy to hear and to describe briefly, that make it a standout among Handel's copious operatic output. This does not mean that these are "the greatest." Indeed, it seems that every time a new recording or video gets issued, some authority will say that the latest discovery ranks with the best. It's a matter of taste, obviously, and yours is as good as anyone's in this respect. Choose with confidence.

I have listed the scoring of each opera[9] because this, more than anything else, shows in the simplest and most graphic terms that no Handel opera sounds exactly like any other. The differences may be subtle, but they are nonetheless significant. In a smallish orchestra, tiny changes often have outsize effects, especially when the composer has Handel's feeling for instrumental color. When viewing the lists, keep in mind that wind instruments could be multiplied at will, and the violins normally played in two parts except where noted. Handel's habit of compositional speed combined with baroque opera's reputation for being formulaic can lead to the impression that his operas are repetitious and lazily conceived. Nothing could be further from the truth.

Agrippina (1709)

Scoring: 2 recorders, 2 oboes, 2 trumpets, timpani, strings (violins in 3 parts, cellos in 2 parts) and continuo.

As you may have noticed, some Handel works are "donors," and others are "receivers." *Agrippina* is a receiver: you might call it the "Greatest Hits of Handel's Italian Period," since very little of the music is original. That doesn't matter, of course, and this black comedy makes a perfect way to hear the young composer at his very best. The story has plenty of sex and decadence (always a plus in opera). The Roman emperors and their families, particularly the demented ones, have never ceased to fascinate. Indeed, you can revisit just about all of these characters from a slightly different perspective in Monteverdi's *L'incoronazione di Poppea,* which can read as a sequel to *Agrippina.* In the Monteverdi, Nero is already emperor and the plot centers on Poppea's ambitions to become empress; *Agrippina* focuses on the title character's machinations to gain the crown for Nero, her son.

Agrippina is Handel's first great female portrait. Scheming and manipulative, loyal to her son Nero but also hopelessly self-centered, she is a splendidly complex creation. Handel gives her some truly remarkable music, especially her great act 2 aria "Pensieri," in which she describes how her thoughts torment her as she begs the gods to assure the success of her plotting. It's a striking setting, literally: the strings jab at Agrippina like a wild animal being prodded with a stick, while the oboe echoes her doubts and despair. The quick "B" section shows a completely different side to her character—strength and determination.

As a listening experience, *Agrippina* is hugely engaging. Most of the arias are short, and the action moves swiftly, as all good comedies must. Even "Pensieri," which packs a huge emotional punch, lasts less than five minutes. If you have time to explore the early cantatas and serenatas you will find much here that is familiar. The works that Handel drew on most heavily for *Agrippina* are:

▪ *Il trionfo del tempo* [oratorio]
▪ *Aminta e Fillide* (a.k.a. *Arresta il passo*) [cantata]
▪ *Clori, Tirsi e Fileno* (a.k.a. *Cor fedele*) [cantata]
▪ *Aci, Galatea e Polifemo* [serenata]

For example, even before turning up intact in *Rinaldo*, Polifemo's gutsy "Sibilar l'angui d'Aletto" provided the basis for the act 2 chorus "Di timpani e trombe," and the strikingly folklike aria "È un foco quel d'amore" from *Aminta e Fillide* appears literally, with the same text, sung by Poppea. The character of Agrippina also features, tragically, in a beautiful and moving solo cantata: *Agrippina condotta a morire* ("Agrippina Led to Her Death"). You may recall from history that after she succeeds in making Nero emperor, he rewards her by having her killed.

As always with Handel, one work leads to others, but I am not suggesting that you lose yourself in a musical jungle, however fun that can be. *Agrippina* has more than enough winning music to savor and enjoy all on its own.

Rinaldo (1711)

Scoring: 3 recorders, 2 oboes, bassoon, 4 trumpets, timpani, strings (violins in 3 parts) and continuo.

Rinaldo is the first of Handel's five "magic" operas, the others being *Amadigi*, *Teseo*, *Orlando*, and *Alcina*. Mythological plots, such as those of *Admeto* and *Atalanta*, not to mention *Semele* and *Hercules*, might also be counted as "magical," but the difference is that in the official batch the magic is integral to the plot, or perhaps more accurately, a meaningful endowment of a specific character, whereas in the mythological stories it's just part of the supernatural order of things.

Baroque operas often take their names from the castrato leads, even when the more interesting characters remain the ladies. In this case, the lady in question is the sorceress and Queen of Damascus Armida, one of the great female roles, and the subject of later operas by Gluck, Haydn, Rossini, and even Dvořák. Most of these stories involve Armida's attempts to seduce Rinaldo away from his crusader's vows, and her sorrow, rage, and vows of vengeance when she fails.

Handel's plot is considerably more complicated, including multiple love interests for the main characters, a Christian magician who gives the crusaders the power to defeat Armida's illusions, Jerusalem under siege, battle music, and plenty of confusion and mistaken identity. In the end, Armida and her original lover, the Saracen king Argante, convert to Christianity, Rinaldo is reunited with his sweetheart Almirena, and everyone celebrates. In later versions the ending is the more familiar one, with the unrepentant and heartbroken Armida flying off in a hellish chariot drawn by dragons.

Handel knew that *Rinaldo* was a "make or break" moment, his first opportunity to prove the viability of Italian opera in England, so he really pulled out all of the stops in terms of costumes, set design, dramatic action, stage machinery, and not the least, the music. The opera is lavishly scored, with (for example) no less than four trumpets, and liberally endowed with arias guaranteed to become "greatest hits." These include not just our old friends "Sibilar gli angui d'Aletto" and "Lascia ch'io pianga," but also Rinaldo's tender "Cara sposa" and his militant "Or la tromba." Armida also gets her share of musical thrills, concluding act 2 with a huge accompanied recitative and two big arias, "Ah! crudel, il pianto mio" and "Vo' far guerra." In short, *Rinaldo* is a feast.

Radamisto (1720)

Scoring: flute, 2 oboes, 2 bassoons, 2 horns, 2 trumpets, strings (cellos in 2 parts) and continuo.

Handel composed *Radamisto* as his first opera for the Royal Academy of Music, a joint stock company that had hired him to manage and produce the London opera season. He was not the only composer employed (others included Ariosti and Bononcini), but he was the leader of the team both musically and organizationally. Technically he was engaged from 1719 to 1734, but the academy was supposed to both (a) produce operas sparing no expense, and (b) turn a profit. As you may have guessed (a) was easily accomplished, (b) not so much. By 1728, the enterprise collapsed, although Handel took over what remained and somehow kept it going through the end of his contract.

Radamisto really tells the story of two faithful women. The first is the title character's beloved wife Zenobia, daughter of King Mitridate of Pontus, who later got a whole Mozart opera to himself. The other is Radamisto's sister, Polissena, who is married to Tiridate, King of Armenia. Radamisto's dad is the king of neighboring Thrace. Tiridate conceives a violent lust for Zenobia and goes to war against Thrace to take her from Radamisto by force. Polissena remains loyal to her husband, however much his infatuation with her sister-in-law causes her to suffer.

To keep things moving for a full three hours, Radamisto and his wife escape Tiridate's siege, but Zenobia hasn't the energy to keep running (or riding) and so she begs her husband to kill her and end the warfare. He tries to stab her, but his heart just isn't in it and so, wounded, she jumps into a river to drown herself. That doesn't work either. Zenobia gets fished out of the water wet, bleeding, and furious, as she's promptly delivered to Tiridate. This offers a terrific opportunity for a couple of acts full of hostile confrontations, especially when Radamisto shows up in disguise and tries to rescue her.

Just when all looks lost, with the bad guy ready to claim victory, Tiridate's army and the populace more generally rebel against him. Now surrounded by enemies, he decides Zenobia's not worth the effort after all and he repents his misdeeds. Polissena gets her husband back (lucky her!); Radamisto and Zenobia remain happily married; Radamisto's dad, who had been taken hostage some time back, is freed; and everyone celebrates the obligatory happy ending with a very substantial concluding chorus.

Radamisto exists in at least three versions, two of which matter. Both contain Radamisto's greatest hit, "Ombra cara," in which he tells his theoretically dead wife's spirit to look forward to his vengeance on Tiridate, after which they will meet again. Originally, the title role was composed for a real soprano, Margherita Durastanti, a close friend from Handel's days in Italy (she also took the lead in *Agrippina*). Six months later, by the end of 1720, Handel had the famous and pricey castrato Senesino on hand for the title role, and Durastanti took over Zenobia (she was, evidently, extremely versatile). Along with a passel of freshly written arias, Handel was able to repeat the opera's initial success with his new cast. Scholars disagree as to the relative merits of the two editions of the score; both have their strong points and we needn't belabor the details here.

Also, both versions have been recorded: April 1720 with Curtis (Virgin/Warner) and the amazing Joyce DiDonato as Radamisto, and December 1720 with McGegan (Harmonia Mundi) and countertenor Ralf Popken taking over Senesino's part, effortlessly. This obvious comparison aside, it's really impossible to choose between them as, again, the differences between editions, conductors, orchestras, and the rest of the cast remain very much a matter of individual taste. Both are worthy, and you can enjoy either without qualms depending on availability.

Ottone (1723)

Scoring: 2 flutes, 2 oboes, 2 bassoons, strings (violins in 3 parts) and continuo.

Otto, King of Germany is the full English title of this piece. His name in Italian sounds a little bit like "Oh, Tony." Although there's a nice battle at the end of act 1, this really is a love story, and the music contains some of Handel's most lyrical writing. The only character who isn't seriously in love with someone is Gismonda, the grasping and ambitious mother of Adelberto, and even she makes time to spare a tender thought for her son ("Vieni, o figlio"). She wants him on the throne of Italy, but Otto is inconveniently on his way to take charge as the country's rightful ruler.

The plan is that Otto will marry Teofane, daughter of the Byzantine emperor, whose brother was exiled for some reason or other and decided to become a pirate under an assumed name. Anyway, Teofane is looking forward to the wedding, having seen a very attractive portrait of the sexy young Otto. Adelberto isn't such a catch, but Gismonda gets him to pretend to be Otto so as to marry Teofane himself. This naturally annoys Matilda, who was, and presumably still is, betrothed to Adelberto.

Many complications ensue, including the imprisonment of Adelberto and his subsequent escape (thanks to Matilda) combined with the attempted kidnapping of Teofane. In act 2 we learn that the abduction isn't going too well thanks to a storm at sea that prevents the boat from leaving—so all of those simile arias about boats and storms and whatnot really have a point. Ultimately all of this gets sorted out, and what we are left with is an opera about love in all of its forms: between husband and wife, mother and son, brother and sister. Handel's scoring is relatively austere: basically just flutes, oboes, and strings, but the textures, sometimes with violins in three parts, are rich and typically seductive. It's no accident that the opera became one of his biggest successes, frequently performed during his lifetime.

Ottone holds a special place in Handel lore for its most famous aria, "Falsa imagine" ("False picture"), in which Teofane sings of her despair on seeing that Adelberto (claiming to be Ottone) looks nothing like his portrait. Handel's prima donna, the temperamental Francesca Cuzzoni—so the story goes—refused to sing it and demanded that Handel give her "a fresh air [aria]," whereupon he grabbed her and threatened to throw her out the window to give her all the "fresh air" she wanted. Needless to say, the aria made her famous in London, and beautiful it is. Cuzzoni specialized in music of a sad or pathetic character, and Handel was more than willing to play to her strengths.

Unfortunately, the situation with recordings is not ideal, and there are no complete videos at this point. The best version of *Ottone* remains McGegan's on Harmonia Mundi, but it may be difficult to find, while the alternative, on Hyperion, features English countertenor James Bowman in the title role. Bowman has the notes, but his tone might be better suited to Ottone's grandmother. His is not a voice, unfortunately, that makes the best case for countertenors as legitimate stand-ins for castratos. This is one opera where it might be best to look for individual numbers on aria recital discs.

Giulio Cesare (1724)

Scoring: 2 recorders, flute, 3 oboes, bassoon, 4 horns, strings (violins in 4 parts, violas and cellos in 2 parts), viola da gamba, theorbo, harp and continuo.

This opera, considered by many to be Handel's greatest, gets the next chapter to itself.

Tamerlano (1724)

Scoring: 2 recorders, 2 flutes, 2 oboes, 2 clarinets, bassoon, strings and continuo.

The three operas *Giulio Cesare*, *Tamerlano*, and *Rodelinda* comprise a trilogy of exceptional quality. Of the three, *Tamerlano* is the darkest and most complex. Although it contains many outstanding individual numbers, and even clarinets in the woodwind section, the overall impression it leaves is of relentless unity—a true ensemble piece. Action, in the form of external events, is minimal. The focus remains squarely on the interactions between the characters. The opera's most telling moment is not an aria, but rather the scene of captive Sultan Bajazet's suicide by poison, which happens mostly onstage and is written into the music in an accompanied recitative, moment by agonizing moment. Because of this scene the entire ending, in fact, really is tragic despite the conventional "happy" resolution. But we are getting a bit ahead of ourselves.

Bajazet has been taken captive by Tamerlano, who wants to marry his daughter Asteria (who in turn is in love with Tamerlano's vassal Andronico). There's no need to go into who loves whom, though, other than to note Bajazet's affection for Asteria—and that is the chaste love between father and daughter. Tamerlano himself is almost uniformly cruel and manipulative, obsessed with power. The action is grim. Act 2, for instance, culminates in the attempted assassination of Tamerlano by Asteria; the third act features one attempted and one successful poisoning. After Bajazet's death, Tamerlano's apparent change of heart and general pardon (it's a bit late for Bajazet) come across as hollow;

and his impending marriage to his original girlfriend Irene, who he callously traded off to Andronico in exchange for Asteria, can't possibly be as happy as he supposes. The stern, minor key tonality of the closing chorus speaks for itself, directly contradicting the plain sense of the words ("love shines brightly," etc.).

Indeed the main characters are mostly, one way or another, monsters. Andronico, torn between love of Asteria and Tamerlano's promise of power, opts for the latter (at least until act 3). Irene will do anything to regain her place as Tamerlano's betrothed. Even Asteria, sweet and lovely as she is supposed to be, spends the better part of two acts plotting the murder of Tamerlano. We may be rooting for her to succeed, but it's certainly not nice. Bajazet, possibly the first great role ever written for the tenor voice, is the true main character, and the only one who engages our sympathy. That's why he has to die, of course. Tamerlano's order that Asteria be sent to his harem, with her father as witness to her humiliation, finally breaks him. Torn between hatred of his foe and concern for his daughter, his helplessness is painful to watch.

Tamerlano's special qualities make it a tough piece to stage convincingly. The story is so monomaniacal, and the characters are so sharply drawn, that it has more the effect of a modern psychological drama than a stylized baroque *opera seria*. The music hits hard—the expression almost too direct. Interestingly, it has been recorded numerous times, with the best version being the most recent: Riccardo Minasi's powerful version for Naïve. The principal glory of the set rests in the presence of two of today's preeminent countertenors, Xavier Sabata and Max Emanuel Cencic, along with noted tenor John Mark Ainsley as Bajazet. It's a cast that's pretty hard to beat. This is not one of those operas you'll probably want to take out and listen to regularly; in this respect it's kind of like Tchaikovsky's harrowing "Pathétique" Symphony. Save it for one of those days when you're really in the mood.

Rodelinda (1725)

Scoring: 2 recorders, flute, 2 oboes, 2 bassoons, 2 horns, strings (violins in 3 parts, violas in 2 parts) and continuo.

Compared to its two immediate predecessors, the situation with recordings of *Rodelinda* is complicated, and so it's best to get that out of the way first. There are two very good videos, Bolton/Farao from Munich with Dorothea Röschmann as a standard-setting Rodelinda, and the opulent Renée Fleming in the Metropolitan Opera production led by Harry Bicket. Those are the ones to get. On CD we basically have Sutherland, way past her prime and using a mangled edition of the score—which wouldn't matter if the performance were great. It's not. Simone Kermes is excellent on Archiv, and so is the rest of the cast, but conductor Alan Curtis, usually so reliable, wimps out on too much of the music. You may not mind when the singing is so fine, but it's a shame nonetheless. Finally, among remaining major label releases, Sophie Daneman (Virgin/Warner) sings quite wonderfully, but Nicholas Kraemer, like Curtis, shortchanges the music's power and expressive range.

As the above suggests, *Rodelinda* is about, well, Rodelinda. It is one of the great roles for a first-rate singing actress. She is a sort of Penelope on steroids, a super noble, heroic, uber-faithful wife. Unbeknownst to her, Bertarido, her theoretically dead husband, is still very much alive. There are also two bad guys in this story, confusingly named Grimoaldo and Garibaldo. The former is yet another of Handel's few great tenor roles, in this case a villain with a conscience. He wants to marry Rodelinda. She pretends to consent as long as he agrees to kill her young son in front of her, knowing full well that he hasn't the guts to do it. And so the plot revolves around a love triangle in which both guys, for different reasons, mistakenly believe her to be unfaithful to them. How Rodelinda resolves these conflicts and manages her eventual reunion with Bertarido forms the gist of the story.

Most *opera seria* plots involve at least two couples, and this one is no exception. Enter Eduige, Grimoaldo's original girlfriend (shades of Irene in the previous opera), determined to win him back or make as much trouble as possible in the process. Then there are the extras unique to this plot, such as Garibaldo, the real villain, and Unulfo, Bertarido's friend. If *Giulio Cesare* offers the ultimate heroes-in-lust opera and *Tamerlano* is a sort of baroque film noir, then *Rodelinda* is a family drama in which virtue triumphs and nobody gets killed except Garibaldo, who certainly has it coming.

Bertarido is the main castrato role, endowed with two of Handel's best arias for Senesino: "Dove sei, amato bene?" ("Where are you, my beloved?"), and "Vivi, tiranno!" ("Live, tyrant!"), but Rodelinda still steals the show. Right from the beginning her opening lament, "Hò perduto il caro sposo" ("I have lost my dear husband"), reveals her depth of character. Many of her arias feature prominently on recital discs, and not just by baroque music specialists. Handel produced one of his most moving sicilianos for Rodelinda, her solo "Ritorna, oh caro e dolce mio tesoro" ("Return, my dear and sweet treasure"), before giving the two lovers one of his finest duets to conclude the second act.

It could be argued that the characters in *Rodelinda* aren't as intrinsically interesting as in the two previous operas. Julius Caesar and Cleopatra, after all, are certainly larger than life, and those in *Tamerlano* suggest that evil can often be more fun than virtue. The emotions and the situations in *Rodelinda* remain human-scaled, but it's precisely for that reason that the music often seems especially affecting. This was the opera selected to start the Handel opera revival in Göttingen, Germany in the 1920s, ostensibly because the heroic effort of Rodelinda to rescue her husband from prison recalls that of Leonore in Beethoven's *Fidelio*. Heroism it seems, no matter how intimately portrayed, is heroism nonetheless.

Admeto (1727)

Scoring: flute, 2 oboes, bassoon, 2 horns, strings (violins in 3 parts) and continuo.

Admeto is *Alceste* in drag. It's tremendous fun. The story of Queen Alceste formed the basis of one of Gluck's most famous "reform" operas—no da capos, no excessive ornamentation, simple text setting, and a stripped down plot. King Admeto lies dying; the oracle has said he can only be saved by the death of someone close to him. Alceste resolves to die in his place, and does so. Hercules goes to Hades to bring her back, and after a lot of dithering about who really ought to be dead the gods grant both Admeto and Alceste life as a reward for their faithfulness and love. That's how it goes, more or less—there are actually several possible endings but we don't need to get into that.

Handel's version of this story required him to take into account "the rival queens:" two prima donnas, Francesca Cuzzoni and Faustina Bordoni, appearing on stage together. If Cuzzoni specialized in pathetic roles, Bordoni made a career out of more buoyant and athletic parts. She specialized in singing repeated notes in rapid tempos, and later married *opera seria* composer par excellence Adolph Hasse (1699–1783). Together, they became *the* operatic power couple of the mid-eighteenth century. Handel wrote five operas in which the two ladies appeared: *Alessandro, Admeto, Riccardo Primo, Siroe*, and *Tolomeo,* and took great care to make sure that each received equal treatment. Note that none of these operas is named after its female lead. That would have been impossible under the circumstances, as you can well imagine, but the women rule nonetheless.

Musical authorities have sniffed at the plots of these operas as being compromised by the requirements of Handel's two leading ladies, with perhaps some truth. However, this is opera, and when you have to choose between some abstract dramaturgical theory and having the two greatest female singers in the world on stage together, what do you think any sane composer would do? So who cares if the plots are a tad creaky now and then? If the singing is great, it doesn't matter. In any event, the two ladies got on relatively well until June 6, 1727, when, egged on by rioting partisans during a performance of Bononcini's *Astianatte,* they had a genuine catfight on stage, to the delight of a scandalized English press. The fact that members of the royal family were in attendance only added to the deliciousness of the thrill.

The principal complications in the plot of *Admeto* concern princess Antigona of Troy, who the king previously dumped to marry Alceste. Learning that the queen is dead and the king recovered from his illness, she shows up disguised and gets a job as a palace gardener in order to figure out how to win him back (and avoid the king's brother, Trasimede, who has been running about drooling over her portrait). Meanwhile, down in Hades, Hercules appears and rescues Alceste. She is worried that Admeto may have found a new love since her death; so she gets Hercules to tell Admeto that, the Underworld being a busy place, he couldn't find her, and she dresses up as a male soldier to give herself some time to survey the situation. This gets us to the middle of act 2, and the rest I am sure you can pretty much guess for yourself.

There is only one major recording of *Admeto*, Curtis/Virgin produced back in 1977, near the dawn of historically informed opera performance. It suffers from a truly terrible casting choice for the title role in the person of countertenor René Jacobs, who turned out to be a much better conductor than he ever was a singer. The leading women, Rachel Yakar and Jill Gomez, aren't bad, but you may be better off with the well sung and directed Göttingen Festival DVD under McGegan. The "East meets West" Japanese production style is trendy and doesn't disgrace the work, even if having Japanese samurai singing about Greek characters is more than a little strange. The same, alas, can't be said of an Arthaus DVD from Halle that sets the story in a modern hospital. You may have more patience (or patients?) for that sort of thing than I do.

Partenope (1730)

Scoring: recorder, 2 flutes, 2 oboes, bassoon, 2 horns, trumpet, strings (violins in 3 parts), viola d'amore, lute or theorbo, drums, and continuo.

Partenope is Handel's first comedy after *Agrippina*, and a brilliant work it is. The opera has been extremely lucky on disc and on video: you really can't go wrong with just about all of the available versions, but forced to choose I would go for the Minasi/Erato, released in 2015 to huge and wholly deserved acclaim. The cast includes soprano Karina Gauvin as Partenope, with countertenor Philippe Jaroussky and normal tenor John Mark Ainsley, among others. It could hardly be more fun. The conventions and plots of *opera seria* often boarder on the silly anyway (see *Admeto*, for example). It only takes a teeny, weeny push to send the whole contrived edifice over the edge into genuine comedy, and

Partenope (pronounced *par-TEN-o-pay*, by the way) exploits this fact at every opportunity.

Partenope is the Queen of Naples, and in the market for a husband. Instead of the usual two competing suitors, she has three: Arsace, confident and swaggering; Armindo, shy but sincere; and Emilio, blustering and militant. Arsace is the main castrato role. A female alto sings Armindo, while Emilio is a tenor. The opera's running gag involves the relationship between Arsace and his ex, Rosmira, who has stalked him all the way to Naples and who appears disguised as the foreign Prince Eurimene. We may scoff at the sexual confusion inherent in *opera seria* casting, but the fact that Arsace, Armindo, and Rosmira/Eurimene are all similar voices gives a certain undeniable plausibility to the ensuing mayhem.

Rosmira's character happily recalls that of the semideranged Donna Elvira in Mozart's *Don Giovanni*: she is obsessively determined to reclaim Arsace's love, but not before she gets her revenge for his having dumped her in the first place. However, Arsace recognizes Rosmira despite the disguise, and tries to prevent her ratting him out to Partenope by claiming his love remains true. She challenges him to prove it by promising never to reveal her actual identity. He agrees, and for the next three acts she proceeds to humiliate him publically, knowing that he can do nothing but stand and take it.

Meanwhile, Emilio has declared war on Partenope because she rejected his amorous advances. In act 2, Armindo saves her life during the battle, but Emilio is captured and Arsace and Rosmira/Eurimene both claim credit for the deed. Rosmira challenges Arsace to a duel to determine which of them is telling the truth, and also (she explains later) because he was unfaithful to his betrothed—Rosmira herself. Arsace is forced to admit the truth of the accusation. Partenope promptly drops him in favor of the brave but quiet Armindo. The duel proceeds with much pageantry, but on the field of battle Arsace insists that the combatants must fight bare-chested. The spectators side with him. This puts Rosmira in a quandary, and forces her to reveal her true identity rather than her breasts. Partenope is suitably impressed. Rosmira gets back her man, appropriately humbled. Emilio, similarly chastened, returns home empty-handed while the two pairs of lovers celebrate their impending marriage.

I am always puzzled by the unwillingness of some commentators to call this opera what it is: a comedy. Winton Dean said much the same thing. Descriptors such as "bittersweet," "semiserious," or "drama with comic elements" constantly crop up in the literature. What are these people afraid of? It's a comedy. More to the point, the work is a *musical* comedy. Like *Agrippina*, this is an ensemble piece, swiftly paced, with generally short arias and recitatives full of witty repartee. While it has no shortage of standout numbers, it needs to be savored in large sections, libretto in hand so that you can enjoy the text—one of the best that Handel ever set. He had known the story for decades before taking it on, and no one can claim that he wasn't up to the job.

Orlando (1733)

Scoring: 2 recorders, 2 oboes, bassoon, 2 horns, strings (violins in 3 parts, cellos in 2 parts, 2 violette marine [violas d'amore]) and continuo.

Now, here is a serious opera with comic elements. It is serious because the threat of harm both to and from Orlando (in English, Roland) is very real, and comic because he's nuts and when his insanity isn't pathetic it's often funny. This was the opera I had in mind when thinking of the title for this chapter: Orlando is driven crazy by sex, he's cured by drugs, and in between everyone gets to sing a lot of really good da capo arias. What's not to love?

Like *Partenope*, *Orlando* also has been very lucky on disc, from the live La Fenice production with Marilyn Horne and conducted by Handel expert Charles Mackerras (Mondo Musica) to the more recent Jacobs starring countertenor Bejun Mehta (Archiv). There's also a fine set from William Christie (Erato), and a historically important version from Christopher Hogwood (L'Oiseau-Lyre) with excellent women—Arleen Auger and Emma Kirkby—but unfortunately the timbrally challenged James Bowman in the title role. And these are only the highlights in a singularly rich discography attesting to the work's enduring popularity on the modern stage.

The plot, such as it is, can be summarized in a single line: Orlando, a knight, goes crazy out of love for Angelica and wreaks havoc until restored to sanity by the wise magician Zoroastro. Handel stuffs this loose framework with as many evocative and affecting arias as it can take. From "Fammi combattere," discussed in chapter 7, to Angelica's haunting "Verdi piante," her farewell to the woods where she fell in love for the first time, the opera is a vocal feast. For Orlando's "sleep" aria, "Già l'ebro mio ciglio" ("Already my eyelids droop"), Handel contrives a magical accompaniment for two solo violette marine. The only problem is that no one knows exactly what a "violetta marina" was, except that it seemed to be a member of the violin family with extra strings that resonate in harmony with the playable strings. Its nearest modern equivalent is the viola d'amore, and so that's the instrument used today.

Perhaps the opera's most famous number, or group of numbers, is Orlando's act 2 mad scene ("Ah! Stigie larve")—you might translate this as "Phantoms of darkness"—a sequence of accompagnatos and ariosos organized in a loose rondo form. Aptly spacy and deranged, it is very different in tone from Dejanira's similarly structured mad scene in *Hercules*. The main theme of the arioso "Vaghe pupille, non piangete" ("Gentle eyes, don't weep") is a distorted gavotte, a medium-slow dance. Dejanira's principal emotion is terror brought on by guilt. Orlando's mad scene is technically madder: it consists mostly of demented babbling, with music of a distracted, tragicomic character.

Finally, the extravagant and fantastical nature of *Orlando*'s plot offers stage producers an extra degree of freedom, for good or ill, to treat the opera as a blank slate on which to try out new interpretive "concepts." Handel always wanted maximum spectacle, nowhere more so than in his operas that include elements of magic and fantasy; but when the main character is crazy, the temptation to go equally nuts with the staging is understandably hard to resist. Putting *Admeto* in a modern hospital is stupid. *Orlando* in a mental ward? Not so much.

Alcina (1735)

Scoring: recorder, 2 flutes, 2 oboes, bassoon, 2 horns, strings (violins in 3 parts, cellos in 2 parts) and continuo.

Alcina is one of those roles made for a true diva. Not only does it require amazing vocal stamina, it encourages a smart singing actress to put her entire being into the portrayal. As a character, she is amazingly complex: proud, loving, sinister, jealous, insecure, tender, sensual, vengeful, and imperious—in short, the total emotional package. Sure, she has this nasty habit of turning her former lovers into rocks, plants, animals, and so forth, but underneath it all she's just your average sorceress looking for love.

Since Joan Sutherland used Alcina as one of her breakout roles (the others were Lucia in Donizetti's *Lucia di Lammermoor* and Violetta in Verdi's *La traviata*), there have been at least three superb modern recordings aside from hers available on major labels: Auger/Hickox (EMI/Warner); Fleming/Christie (Erato/Warner); and DiDonato/Curtis (Archiv). Any of them do the work proud. Sutherland's features great singing but the edition, prepared and conducted by her husband, Richard Bonynge, is relentlessly, if often delightfully, "inauthentic." There are several videos as well, and most share casts with the same folks who made the audio-only recordings, so collectors are spoiled for choice.

Interestingly, in all of these productions the male castrato lead, the knight Ruggiero, is not sung by a countertenor, but rather by an excellent female vocalist: Teresa Berganza for Bonynge, Della Jones for Hickox, Susan Graham for Christie, and Maite Beaumont for Curtis. This matters because the character of Ruggiero is almost as important as that of Alcina, and his part is, for a Handelian castrato, unusually varied expressively. Indeed, he gets what is arguably the most beautiful and famous aria in the entire opera: "Verdi prati," or "Green meadows." But then, all of the characters have great moments. Alcina's sister Morgana concludes the first act with an aria so delicious, "Tornami a vagheggiar" ("Look on me tenderly"), that Sutherland's Alcina took it over, just to keep the "donna prima."

The plot turns on a clever gimmick. As soon as Alcina realizes that she truly loves Ruggiero, her magic deserts her. She begins the opera brimming with confidence and sensual swagger. However, by the time we get to her great act 2 accompanied recitative and aria, "Ah, Ruggiero crudel/Ombre pallide" ("Ah, cruel Ruggiero/Pale shadows"), and culminating in her final pathetic siciliano "Mi restano le lagrime" ("My tears remain"), her sadness and frustration become overwhelming. That said, although Alcina may be a sympathetic "bad guy," bad she remains. Ultimately fate catches up with her and she fades away along with all of her enchantments and illusions. There is no last minute repentance or redemption.

The closing scene is genuinely touching nonetheless. After Alcina and Morgana vanish into the ground, all of her former lovers get turned back into their human selves and Ruggiero returns to the embrace of Bradamante, his true love. Handel had Marie Sallé's dance troupe on hand for *Alcina*, as with *Ariodante*, so the opera includes dance sequences in strategic places—most notably during the final transformation, where the music provides a perfect counterpart to the happenings on stage.

Serse (*Xerxes*) (1738)

Scoring: 2 recorders, 2 oboes, bassoon, 2 horns, trumpet, strings (violins in 3 parts) and continuo.

Serse, king of Persia, is so easily besotted that he sings a love song ("Ombra mai fu") to his plane tree, but so fickle that the second he sees Romilda he dumps the tree and decides to marry her. Now if this were a true *opera seria*, the plane tree would turn out to be Serse's original betrothed in disguise, and after singing a lament or a vengeance aria she would spend the reminder of the work wreaking havoc in an effort to win him back. She would also have to fend off the advances of Serse's exiled brother—let's call him Archimedio—who has secretly returned as a lumberjack, with potentially lethal consequences. But because this is a comedy we are spared these complexities. The description of the opera by my colleague Robert Levine is so apt that it deserves to be quoted in full:

> Serse is a great opera, filled with terrific arias and a followable plot. There's plenty of room for in-love pain and anguish from Romilda and Arsamene (Serse's brother) who love each other, Princess Amastre, who Serse has dumped in favor of Romilda (who doesn't love him), and Atalanta, who loves Arsamene. But there's great humor and irony as well: Serse changes his mind like a spoiled brat, and his protestations of love are brief and whimsical (in fact, he falls in love with Romilda on the spot, after hearing her sing!); Atalanta seems to get great joy out of spitefully playing the being-in-love game. Arsamene's servant, Elvino, is a goofball (the only totally comic character in any Handel opera), while Ariodate, a soldier in Serse's army and the father of Romilda and Atalanta, is an idiot. Amastre's disguise in male clothing to get revenge on Serse adds to the intrigue.

Okay, maybe this really is an *opera seria*, but one with its tongue kept firmly in its cheek. The music sparkles. There's much more to it than "Ombra mai fu." At this point in his career, Handel would compose only two more original operas, and while hardly experimental, these last works do show him stretching the boundaries of the medium in an effort to give his audience something new and keep them coming to the theater. The fact that it didn't work says nothing about the quality of the music that he actually composed. Handel switched to oratorio to follow the money, not because he ever tired of writing operas.

The music of *Serse* is often remarkably continuous, the interplay between recitative, aria, and arioso increasingly fluid. There's a new aria type here: the arietta, or "little aria," similar to the cavatina (arioso) in that it avoids the usual ABA format. All told, *Serse* contains forty solo songs. Of these, Handel calls twenty-four "aria," eight "arioso," and eight "arietta." Romilda's closing solo, leading to the final chorus, is not an aria, but an accompanied recitative. There are also three duets, and three choruses not counting the one at the end. They are true choruses, not merely numbers for the soloists singing together. Atalanta's act 2 aria "Dirà che amor" ("He will say that love") has an "A" section consisting of a full ABA, da capo form, but in miniature. The "B" section is a brief secco recitative, whereas the return of "A" is the same da capo, but with a different text.

Serse, in short, is full of surprises and fresh ideas, all of them dictated by the pace and point of the action. Although the opera lasts just a few minutes short of three hours, you'd never know it. The music really moves. Christie's recording for EMI/Warner (formerly Virgin Classics), starring mezzo-soprano Anne-Sophie von Otter, soprano Sandrine Piau, and countertenor Lawrence Zazzo, is the one to get. *Serse* (as *Xerxes*) is also one of only two Handel operas—the other is *Giulio Cesare*—available in full score in an inexpensive but nicely printed Dover edition. Even if your ability to read music is limited, you can learn a lot just by following along and seeing what Handel actually wrote and how the singers embellish the vocal lines. You may want to give it a shot.

This concludes our "baker's dozen" survey of Handel operas. Although there are so many more, you can see that these pieces often lead naturally to works that we haven't discussed in detail because they fall naturally into groups: the "magic" operas, for example, or "the rival queens." There were the operas composed for the Royal Academy, and the later group for Covent Garden. Three of the four works written between *Rinaldo* and *Radamisto*—*Il pastor fido (1712), Teseo (1713),* and *Amadigi di Gaula (1715)*—also form a natural cluster well worth exploring. There are operas on historical subjects, and operas with mythological backgrounds. Perhaps most fun are those pieces featuring characters like Armida and Alceste, who appear in works by different composers in different periods, inviting comparison.

One last group of works I do want to draw particular attention to, however, is the pasticcios. A pasticcio is what you get when you assemble an entire opera consisting of preexisting music, adapted to a new libretto. Often the arias don't need to be changed at all because they are not individualized—they don't mention specific characters, or if they do it's no big deal to switch out the names. Simile arias are particularly handy in this respect, and this provides one explanation for the fact that baroque operas have recourse to them so frequently. Secco and accompanied recitatives, naturally, would have to be newly composed around the different plot, but that is mostly a simple task.

Handel created two kinds of pasticcio: ones featuring music by multiple composers, and ones consisting only of his own works. In this latter category, as the list at the head of this chapter shows, there are three titles: *Oreste*, *Alessandro severo*, and *Giove in Argo*, the latter only reconstructed and given its modern premiere in 2006. The pasticcios tend to get ignored because they contain little original music (Handel wasn't above adding a new number or two, if necessary) and, as we well know, there is a strong prejudice in favor of unique works. "Big deal," I hear you say. "Isn't almost everything Handel wrote a pasticcio in some measure?" Right you are. It's simply a matter of degree. There is no inherent qualitative difference between these three operas and any others, either musically or dramatically.

Indeed, you could argue that in terms of musical quality the pasticcios are *better*, at least potentially, to the extent that Handel selected his most outstanding numbers for inclusion within them. *Oreste*, for example, contains music mostly from *Radamisto, Floridante, Ottone, Tamerlano, Riccardo Primo, Siroe, Lotario, Partenope*, and *Sosarme*. It is both a self-contained drama that stands perfectly well on its own, and a selection of highlights from those prior works. So, if you don't have time for nine separate operas, you can hear samples from all of them, and a good story to boot, just by spending a scant two and half hours with *Oreste*. Happily, all three pasticcios have now been recorded, and quite well, too (for MD&G under George Petrou and Virgin/Warner with Alan Curtis). Don't let the bad press they have received historically dissuade you from trying them.

Aria Recitals and Collections

If you want to enjoy Handel's operas and oratorios but can't spare the time to sit through complete works, aria recitals by individual singers offer an excellent place to start. That said, I was surprised to read, in the late Christopher Hogwood's otherwise very fine Handel biography, the following unfortunate lines:

> One particular fad that has dominated recent Handel record-
> ing projects is the aria recital: anthologies of arias intended to
> display the showcased soprano or countertenor in a selection of
> their favorite numbers. The result can be exhilarating with an
> experienced baroque singer and a flowing programme (Sandrine
> Piau with Rousset, Emma Kirkby with Goodman), but all too
> often these recital discs contain predictable selections and offer
> very little other than an opportunity to massage the singer's ego.
> Perhaps that in itself is a peculiarly authentic element with which
> Handel's celebrated castrati and prima donnas would have sympa-
> thized, but a steady stream of vanity recitals (including "Ombra
> mai fu," "Lascia ch'io pianga" and "Where'er you walk" which
> show little regard for which voice Handel originally intended
> them or for the dramatic context of the words) does not do the
> composer justice.[10]

Oh dear, where to start? First off, Hogwood's is one of the very few general biographies to pay at least minimal attention to recordings, and good for him. His praise of recitals by Piau (Naïve) and Kirkby (Hyperion) is wholly justified, and I second his recommendations enthusiastically. Naturally he has an agenda: to promote "historically informed performance," mostly by his colleagues but implicitly his own as well. There is absolutely nothing wrong with that, but the straw man argument that he constructs here just won't wash.

There is a singular elitism, even arrogance, standing behind Hogwood's avowed concern for "authenticity" and doing "justice" to the composer when what he means, obviously, is the achievement of those goals as he chooses to define them. Hogwood's recording of *Athalia*, for example, is hardly an objective treatise on correct period performance style, however much he might wish it were. It stars Joan Sutherland, no less, and represents his own very personal interpreta-tion—one over which he exercises vastly more control than any con-ductor in Handel's time ever would or could. Recitals, in any case, are by definition as much about the singer as the composer. If the soloist chooses to highlight a single composer specifically, well and good, but that is still the artist's prerogative.

There is absolutely nothing that a modern vocal recitalist would do to any Handel role that is worse than what the composer himself did willingly on any given day. Laying the blame for the practice of arranging the music to suit the singer solely on the vanity or caprice of star castratos and prima donnas presupposes that Handel's conception of a work was unalterably graven in stone from the start, when we know that this is not true. No one was more stubborn than Handel when it came to dealing with recalcitrant singers (remember his threatened defenestration of Cuzzoni over "Falsa imagine" in *Ottone*), but at the same time no one treated his own works more flexibly in order to let his cast shine and hopefully succeed with the public.

Most aria collections will include popular favorites. That's partly what sells them; but I have never seen a modern recital of the type that Hogwood castigates, and he conveniently fails to specify any examples. Take Marilyn Horne's classic Handel program (Erato) for instance. In its latest incarnation it includes five arias from *Rinaldo*, plus numbers from *Serse* (yes, "Ombra mai fu"), *Partenope*, *Orlando*, and *Agrippina*. There are a few arias by Vivaldi as well, as a bonus. Mexican tenor Rolando Villazón's idiosyncratic Handel program on DG transposes several castrato arias, including "Ombra mai fu" and Ariodante's "Scherza infida," to fit the tenor register, but he does so with the complicity of early music specialist Paul McCreesh and his period instrument ensemble. If you dislike the timbre of your average countertenor, as many listeners do, hearing this music sung by a true tenor can prove a blessing.

Or consider Renée Fleming's Handel recital on Decca. Fleming is not a baroque specialist, and her natural vocal opulence does not sit well with modern theories of baroque timbre (which no one alive can confirm in any case). She does give us "Ombra mai fu" plus "Lascia ch'io pianga," but these are just two of sixteen tracks, including arias from *Semele*, *Scipione*, *Orlando*, *Samson*, *Giulio Cesare*, *Rodelinda*, *Lotario*, *Agrippina*, and *Alexander Balus*. Some of them are very rarely heard. On what basis should we deny her the right to sing them as beautifully as she does?

The bottom line is that there are many ways to "do the composer justice." An intelligently planned recital is certainly one of them, but it does not take precedence over great singing, which *always* does the composer justice no matter the circumstances. Furthermore, what for Hogwood might be an aesthetic abomination or a tired warhorse could very well be a new listener's happy introduction to Handel. I am as big a fan as anyone of listening to complete works played from scholarly editions, in as appropriate a musical style as we know how to produce, but who are we to suggest that there is only one true path that everyone must follow? The main purpose in listening, after all, is personal entertainment and enjoyment—not to pay worshipful homage to the shade of some long-dead composer.

Many of the tracks on the accompanying CD, including arias by Lucy Crowe, Andreas Scholl, Bejun Mehta, Lisa Saffer, and Lorraine Hunt, come from recital discs on Harmonia Mundi. One of their more successful programming concepts is a four-disc series called "Arias for . . . ," individual discs grouped around works composed for specific singers: Cuzzoni (Lisa Saffer, soprano), Durastante (Lorraine Hunt, mezzo soprano), Senesino (Drew Minter, countertenor for castrato), and Montagnana (David Thomas, bass). Equally fine individual discs from the same label include "As steals the morn . . . ," a lovely program of arias and scenes from opera and oratorio for tenor (sung by Mark Padmore). Many recordings mix the arias up with instrumental pieces to provide extra variety.

I also recommend a very special disc featuring the exquisite Dorothea Röschmann singing Handel's Nine German Arias. These are not opera at all, but chamber music for soprano, violin (or flute, or oboe), and continuo. Even though not composed as a unified cycle, the songs naturally comprise a mini-recital all their own, lasting about fifty minutes in total. The texts, by our friend Mr. Brockes, come from an immense, multivolume set of religious poetry called *The Pleasures of Earthly Life in God*. If that doesn't sum up Handel's aesthetic in a nutshell, then nothing does. He responded vividly not just to the spiritual content of the words, but also to the poet's extensive use of nature imagery and the optimistic tone. Brockes himself knew these settings and thought very highly of them. Of course, some of the music did find its way into the operas and larger vocal works, especially *Giulio Cesare, Tamerlano,* and *Rodelinda,* but then we would expect no less. Although composed in the mid-1720s these pieces, Handel's last works in German, were only published two hundred years later. Until then, they circulated only in manuscript copies.

Two splendidly sung but very different discs by star singers include mezzo soprano Magdalena Kožená's oddly accented (in the English numbers) but otherwise aptly programmed Handel recital for Archiv, and bass-baritone Bryn Terfel's grab-bag selection—including transposed castrato originals—on Deutsche Grammophon (DG). Both mix opera and oratorio arias and both feature accompaniments in the best modern period instrument style. Kožená has the Venice Baroque Orchestra under Andrea Marcon, while the late Charles Mackerras, dean of the modern Handel revival, joins Terfel along with the Scottish Chamber Orchestra.

Terfel's disc would probably find Hogwood spinning in his grave—though Christopher Purves's enterprising collection of bass arias for Hyperion surely would earn an enthusiastic endorsement. Less dogmatic listeners will find Terfel full of good-natured energy and warmth. Kožená, on the other hand, has recorded a lot of Handel, including a fine disc of solo cantatas, a stunning Cleopatra in *Giulio Cesare,* and the soprano arias on one of the worst ever recordings of *Messiah,* all with Minkowski. This latter disaster is the conductor's fault.

If you want to hear what some of today's notable countertenors are up to, consider David Daniels's Handel aria collection on Warner/Erato. His "Ombra mai fu" is one of the best, and if you enjoy aria recitals you just have to resign yourself to owning dozens of versions; it is the Pachelbel *Canon* of Handel arias, and there's no way around it. Max Emanuel Cencic on Warner/Virgin sings a boldly chosen program of mezzo-soprano arias from such rarely heard works as *Imeneo, Arianna, Amadigi, Floridante,* and *Parnasso in Festa.* Finally, don't overlook Xavier Sabata's cleverly assembled portrait of Handel's villains on *Bad Guys* (Aparte). It's a terrific concept, especially since we know that the bad guys have all the fun.

Finally, there are plenty of brilliant recitals by some of the best Handel specialists and baroque singers of our day. These include Joyce DiDonato's *Furore* (Warner/Virgin), an amazing collection of arias sung by damsels in distress. Her "Where shall I fly" from *Hercules* is a real scorcher. French soprano Natalie Dessay smartly collects most of Cleopatra's arias from *Giulio Cesare* into a single program that, interspersed with some instrumental numbers and including the final duet, forms a very highly satisfying recital all by itself (Warner/ Erato). Sandrine Piau and Sara Mingardo get together with Rinaldo Alessandrini and his Concerto Italiano for an appealing assortment of arias and duets on Naïve. Lastly, the lovely Amanda Forsythe explores *The Power of Love* on Avie, joined by the Cleveland baroque ensemble Apollo's Fire.

This is just a sample of a true discographic bonanza. There are collections for every taste: opera arias, oratorio arias (not forgetting Karina Gauvin on Atma), and combinations of both. I haven't even mentioned first-rate recitals featuring multiple composers—discs by Cecilia Bartoli, for example, or Vivica Genaux. There are "concept" albums focused on an overriding theme, and those simply comprising a portrait of the singer. Some have accompaniments including period instruments, others prefer modern ensembles, but all give at least some consideration to historically informed performance practice. This generally means keeping tempos lively, rhythms sharp, ornamentation appropriate, and a colorful and smart handling of the continuo. We truly are spoiled for choice, and it's hard to go wrong.

Handel aria recitals existed in Handel's own century as well, particularly as benefit concerts for individual singers. One particularly memorable event took place on Thursday, May 27, 1784, in connection with the commemoration of the twenty-fifth anniversary of the composer's death. An orchestra of 138 players joined a vast chorus and necessary soloists for a selection of opera arias and oratorio choruses (plus a few overtures and concertos). It's fascinating to see what pieces contemporary audiences found most attractive. So, let's wrap up this section with the list of arias played that evening:

- "Sorge infausta" (*Orlando*)
- "Rendi 'l sereno" (*Sosarme*)
- "Caro, vieni" (*Riccardo primo*)
- "Va tacito e nascosto (*Giulio Cesare*)
- "M'allontano sdegnose pupille" (*Atalanta*)
- "Dite, che fa" (*Tolomeo*)
- "Vi fida lo sposo (*Ezio*)
- "Alma del gran Pompeo" (accompanied recitative from *Giulio Cesare*)
- "Affani del pensier" (*Ottone*)
- "Nasce al bosco" (*Ezio*)
- "Io t'abbraccio" (duet from *Rodelinda*)
- "Ah! Mio cor!" (*Alcina*)

A couple of points are worth mentioning. First, these arias were chosen at a time when none of Handel's operas was still being performed. The notion of fidelity to complete works is very much a modern concept. It's a good one, by and large, but let's not kid ourselves about its necessity or inevitability. Second, many of the arias come from operas that remain quite rarely heard: *Ezio, Riccardo primo, Sosarme, Tolomeo,* and *Atalanta*. This suggests (and I hope you're not surprised) that even little-known Handel contains many gems worth discovering. So, feel free to mix and match, listen as you please, and put together your own aria programs. Handel wouldn't have minded at all.

In considering Handel's operas as a whole, it's worth stressing by way of conclusion just how remarkable his achievement was. You don't wake up one day and say, "I am going to make a living writing operas as a foreigner in a country with no tradition of the medium, for an audience that doesn't understand the language, and which looks upon the whole enterprise with suspicion, if not downright hostility." Yet this is just what Handel attempted. He never explained his thinking, but for whatever reason he saw a niche in English musical life that he felt prepared to occupy, and occupy it did. But there must be more to it than just his desire to earn his keep.

Ultimately, despite all of the risk and uncertainty, the grief and aggravation that running an opera company entails, you've just got to love it, unconditionally, with a consuming passion. Nothing else really explains how Handel was able to pull himself back from the brink of ruin, time after time, and emerge triumphant. It is said that he never expressed any bitterness when a work failed to please or played to empty houses. If true, this can only be because he truly was doing what he loved most.

Channeling Cleopatra
Musical Characterization

The success of any opera over the long term depends on the composer's ability to create believable characters. However, in this context "believable" means something very specific: *emotionally true*. It could hardly be otherwise, given the fact that few operatic characters are "normal" people, and the situations that they find themselves in are, more often than not, fantastical, hopelessly contrived, or just plain preposterous. None of these matter, however, if the characters react to their circumstances and to each other credibly, amplified and made manifest through music of genuine expressive depth. In other words, you feel the emotional truth directly and immediately, in your gut, conveniently bypassing the killjoy exercise of rational thought.

Consider an especially crazy, but for that reason vivid, example. Polifemo, who we met in the serenata *Aci, Galatea e Polfemo*, is a Cyclops—not the most relatable of characters, I'm sure you'll agree. Having been soundly rejected by Galatea for reasons that no sane person would question, he sings the self-pitying aria "Fra l'ombre e gl'orrori." Here is the English translation of the text:

Amidst the shadows and horrors
The dazed butterfly,
Never can play
When the flame is spent;
So it is that the fears,
Of this deluded soul
Can never have peace,
Nor hope for pleasure.

Not only is the comparison of a Cyclops to a confused butterfly absurd, but Handel concocts a musical setting that is as evocatively maudlin as the text, with flutes in the orchestra standing in for the butterflies, and huge vocal leaps combined with impossibly low bass notes driving home an almost physical portrait of the character. It's a wonderful aria, comical, but also—and here's the point—genuine. I mean, can you possibly imagine a move convincing musical embodiment of a Cyclops's lovelorn misery? And if music can make Polifemo's grotesque anguish believable, then it can do anything.

This example, though, is only a snapshot, a single moment in which Polifemo expresses a single feeling. To round out the portrait of the character you need more, and varied, feelings, and so more arias. We can expect the expressive vocabulary of a Cyclops to be relatively limited, and so it is—even more so in the English version of this same story, as previously noted. Real, sympathetic people are more complex, and require more time to develop. That's one of the reasons that operas tend to be long; not so much because the plots are tangled, but because the emotions that they engender take time to develop and emerge.

Giulio Cesare is probably Handel's longest opera, lasting just a few minutes shy of four hours. Orchestrally it is also his most lavish, with four horns, harp, viola da gamba—just have a look at the scoring listed in the previous chapter. It has five major characters: Cesare (Caesar), Cleopatra, her brother Tolomeo (Ptolemy), Cornelia, widow of the murdered Pompeo (Pompey), and Sesto (Sextus), her young son. Caesar and Ptolemy are castrato roles, whereas Sextus was written for soprano Margherita Durastanti. Not all of the principals enjoy equal importance, but Handel intends to draw credible portraits of them all, and that means a lot of arias in which they get to express a very wide range of feelings. The central protagonists are Caesar and Cleopatra, and arguably Cleopatra is the most important of all. Certainly, the story gives her the farthest expressive journey to travel.

Her part is huge. Not counting secco recitative, it consists of eight arias, two accompagnatos, and one duet. Handel endows the role of Caesar similarly. As I said, it's a long opera. This gives Handel plenty of room to explore his characters, and with a gripping story about sex, conquest, and politics, there's no shortage of opportunities. We will find Cleopatra's personality, then, expressed mainly in her arias. Since all of them are either da capos or dal segnos—that is, they have an ABA shape—each potentially offers two revealing moments, one of which (the "A" section) you get to hear twice. Summarizing the plot and taking each of Cleopatra's solos in turn, we can discover how Handel creates one of his most complete and fascinating characters.

Here is the entire role in outline. Don't worry about the Italian—all of the texts will be translated as we come to them.

1. "Non disperar; chi sà?"
2. "Tutto può donna vezzosa"
3. "Tu la mia stella sei"
4. "V'adoro, pupille"
5. "Venere bella"
   "Che sento? oh Dio!" [accompagnato]
6. "Se pietà di me non senti"
7. "Piangerò la sorte mia"
   "Voi, che mie fide ancelle" [accompagnato]
8. "Da tempeste il legno infranto"
   "Caro! più amabile beltà" [duet]

The opera begins with a murder. Caesar arrives in Egypt to general acclaim, as a conqueror. The wife (Cornelia) and son (Sextus) of vanquished general Pompey plead for clemency, which Caesar grants. His act of generosity is forestalled, however, by the arrival of a messenger from Ptolemy, joint ruler of Egypt with his sister Cleopatra. The messenger brings as a gift the head of Pompey, murdered at Ptolemy's command. Caesar is horrified, Cornelia faints, and Sextus swears vengeance. When Cornelia revives, the Roman tribune Curio, aide to Caesar, offers to marry her on the spot. She tells him to get lost.

The scene shifts to a room in the Egyptian royal palace. Cleopatra says, to paraphrase Mel Brooks, "It's great to be the queen." She receives the dismaying news that her idiot brother has just mucked things up with Caesar by killing Pompey. She resolves to use her feminine charms to beguile the Roman conqueror and secure her own position on the throne. After a nasty spat with Ptolemy, she reveals her intentions in her first aria, "Non disperar; chi sà?"

A
Do not despair. Who knows?
You may have the same luck in reigning that you already have in
love.

B
Looking at your beauty,
You will find there the way to win over a heart.

Handel's setting of this aria is chirpy and buoyant, establishing
Cleopatra as a scheming coquette, confident and rather shallow. The
"A" section employs Handel's typical fast ending—a quick descending octave snap. Since the text consistently focuses on Cleopatra's
determination to use her physical attractions to realize her political
ambitions, the "B" section represents only a small contrast in tone.
The aria is relatively short, a bit more than three bubbly minutes. It
serves not only to introduce Cleopatra, but also to create maximum
contrast with the dark opening scenes, making her personality shine
even brighter.

Meanwhile, back in the palace, Ptolemy has heard of Caesar's
anger at his "gift." Insulted, he plots with his lieutenant Achilla to kill
Caesar, promising that once the dastardly deed is done Achilla can
have Cornelia as his wife. Over in Caesar's camp, a ceremony honor-
ing Pompey is in progress. Cleopatra approaches Caesar, disguised as a
distressed woman named Lydia. She says that Ptolemy, that miscreant,
has robbed her of her status and her fortune. She demands justice and
Caesar, falling instantly in lust, tells her that she shall have it as soon as
he goes to the palace. He departs and Cleopatra, delighted, celebrates
her success in her second aria, "Tutto può donna vezzosa:"

A
Anything is possible for a pretty woman
If she opens her mouth or turns her gaze with the promise of
love.

B
Every shot will pierce a breast
If the shooter of the dart has no flaws.

The words of this aria might lead us to believe that it's much the same as Cleopatra's first number, but the music says otherwise. Rhythmically, the ritornello is extremely complex, with echo effects and syncopations galore. Cleopatra's repeated, two note yelps on the word "tutto" ("anything") show us her delight, but the unpredictability of the vocal line confirms just what a sly customer she really is. In other words, she has brains behind her looks. The "B" section, too, is far more serious than previously, its minor key shading not so much dark as determined, and at five and a half minutes this is a much more substantial piece, overall.

To further confirm the impression we now have of Cleopatra's character, Cornelia and Sextus enter immediately following her aria. Cornelia wants to grab a sword to kill Ptolemy, but Sextus insists he will do the job. Cleopatra, still disguised as Lydia, overhears the whole conversation. She introduces herself to the grieving pair and offers her servant, Nirenus, as a guide to the palace—and off they go, full of gratitude. With this backup plan in place, Cleopatra relaxes in anticipation of her victory with the lilting, folklike, triple-time aria "Tu la mia stella sei," which requires no special comment. Here are the words:

A
Be my lucky star, dear hope,
And let my desires find a great and handsome success.

B
We soon shall see the steady faithfulness that is in this heart.
And what love can accomplish.

This is the last we shall hear of Cleopatra until act 2. In the closing scenes of the first act, Caesar and Ptolemy finally meet and insult each other, and Cornelia and Sextus turn up to challenge Ptolemy to mortal combat. He calls his guards and orders them to lock up Sextus and send Cornelia to his harem to work as a gardener, keeping her on ice for Achilla (who he intends to betray so he can have Cornelia for himself—she's a hot commodity). As they are led off, Achilla promises to free them if Cornelia consents to marry him. Needless to say she declines, and the act concludes with a siciliano duet of farewell for mother and son, certainly one of the most stunningly beautiful and sad duets Handel ever penned.

The opening scene in act 2 answers the tricky baroque question: How do you write a love scene when you can't show anything? Handel does it with music—shamelessly succulent, erotic music. Cleopatra, a.k.a. Lydia, prepares her seduction by arranging a meeting with Caesar in a cedar grove decorated to show Mount Parnassus in the background with the Palace of Virtue on its slopes. A separate stage orchestra, consisting of oboe, two violins, viola, viola da gamba, harp, theorbo, bassoons and cello, plays in the background. All the violins, on stage and in the orchestra, are muted, and the dusky tone of the viola da gamba sounds muted whether it is or not.

The melody of the stage band anticipates that of Cleopatra's aria, so that when she appears, dressed (ironically, I suppose) as Virtue, and surrounded by the nine Muses, the tune that she sings ("V'adoro, pupille") comes as the fulfillment of the music already heard:

A
I adore you, eyes, which are the stings of love.
Your sparks pierce my soul.

B
My sorrowful heart begs for your pity,
And every hour calls you its dearly beloved.
[Caesar: There is not even in heaven a melody similar to such a beautiful song.]

As so often with Handel, special circumstances call for a unique handling of otherwise standard forms. The "A" section is as sensual a love song as can be found anywhere; while "B" is a single, darkly yearning phrase interrupted by Caesar's excited exclamation in secco recitative. With the repeat of A, the seduction is complete and Lydia vanishes, much to Caesar's dismay. Cleopatra's servant then pops up and invites the disconsolate Caesar to visit "Lydia" in her apartment to discuss Ptolemy's treachery, and presumably other matters. Caesar responds with an enthusiastic, earthy, pastoral simile aria comparing Lydia to a bird (cue for solo violin). The two voices intertwine vigorously, leaving no doubt, musically at least, of further intertwining to come. And that, my friends, is sex, baroque style.

The next scene, or group of scenes, moves the plot along smartly and contains arias for Achilla, Ptolemy, Cornelia, and Sextus, in that order. Cornelia is working in the garden mulching as Achilla sexually harasses her. Suddenly Ptolemy shows up and tells him to go kill Caesar, as he promised. After Achilla leaves, Ptolemy takes over the sexual harassment of Cornelia, with little success: she threatens to tear his heart out. This angers him greatly, and he sings a really vicious "bad guy" aria about taking her by force if she won't come to him willingly. He storms out.

No sword being handy, Cornelia decides to kill herself by jumping off of the seraglio's walls and letting herself be devoured by wild beasts. Sextus comes to her rescue, having been freed by Cleopatra's servant Nirenus. Together, they plot to conceal Sextus in the harem so that when Ptolemy comes alone to take his lascivious pleasures Sextus can ambush and dispatch him. Cornelia gets the obligatory aria about how a steersman in a stormy sea never gives up hope—actually, that's just the "B" section—while Sextus responds with his own simile aria, "L'angue offeso mai reposa," one of the opera's many highlights, explaining how an angry snake never stops striking its prey until it has run out of venom.

This is a great piece, and a popular recital item by itself. It also shows that Handel expected a large string section in his operas. The accompaniment is very full, and with a large ensemble the music surges with the necessary elemental force. Too many modern performances settle for pint-size, "authentic" string sections, but if you hear a great performance with a substantial numbers of players, such as Minkowski's with Anne Sofie von Otter as Sextus, there's a world of difference. Handel himself had a sizeable string section numbering some twenty-five players. Minkowski uses about thirty-two, the difference being mostly additional violas and cellos.

Over in the pleasure garden, Cleopatra awaits her rendezvous with Caesar, admitting to herself for the first time that she has fallen in love with him. Still, she wants to make sure that he feels similarly. In her gracious and very catchy aria "Venere bella," she prays she will inspire in him as much love as she feels.

A
Lovely Venus, for an instant grant,
Endow me with all the graces of the god of love.

B
You must have perceived that my appearance
Should inspire passion in a royal heart.

She feigns sleep so that she can hear Caesar's reaction when he arrives. That works too well. Salivating over her supine form, he murmurs that if he gets really lucky, perhaps her feelings for him would be so strong as to make her want to become his wife. Cleopatra bounces up and says, "I do." Caesar reproaches her for harboring such thoughts as a vassal of Cleopatra (remember, she's still "Lydia" to him). She responds teasingly, saying that if she disgusts him when awake, then she'll just go back to sleep. Suddenly, Curio rushes in and says that a group of conspirators is on the way to kill Caesar. There's a good bit of back-and-forth that follows, the upshot of which is that Cleopatra inadvertently reveals herself and her true feelings to Caesar. She tries bravely to use her authority as queen to stop the plot but to no avail. She begs Caesar to flee. Naturally he refuses, singing one of those "off we go to battle" arias that were a specialty of castratos everywhere.

This leaves a devastated Cleopatra behind to express her fears and sadness in her accompanied recitative and aria "Se pietà di me non senti," which you can hear on the accompanying CD. Out of her first five arias, four have been quick, none have been sad, and the previous slow one, "V'adoro pupille," is what they call a "set piece," a song that is part of the plot. It doesn't reveal anything personal about Cleopatra other than her sexiness. Here, then, we encounter the first expression of her innermost feelings in a slow tempo, and Handel makes the most of it. You might say that the accompanied recitative accumulates tension, while the aria releases it in an outpouring of emotion:

Accompagnato:
What do I hear? O God! Let Cleopatra die as well.

Wretched soul, what are you saying? Ah, be quiet!
To avenge myself I will join this combat with the face of Bellona
and the heart of Mars.
Meanwhile, o gods, you who rule in heaven,
Protect my beloved, who remains the comfort and hope of my
heart.

Aria:

A
If you don't feel pity for me,
Righteous heaven, I will die.

B
You must give peace to my torments,
Or this soul will expire.

Thematically, this aria bears a strong family resemblance to "Scherza infida" from *Ariodante*. Together with its preceding recitative it lasts about ten minutes, making it the longest single number in the entire opera (the recitative only takes about a minute). There is one other subtlety worth mentioning. The aria's ritornello is only seven bars long, an odd number. Whether you notice it consciously or not, this makes the music feel unbalanced, with the voice entering a bar too early. Similarly, the dal segno repeat cuts the ritornello down to only three bars, ratcheting up Cleopatra's tension still further. This is just one of those little touches that distinguishes a master from a hack.

Act 2 draws to a close in Ptolemy's harem. Cornelia is with him. He puts his sword on a table so it doesn't get in the way of his haremizing, and Sextus jumps out to seize it. Suddenly Achilla shows up, takes the sword, and rather than doing the obvious and killing Sextus, he tells Ptolemy that Caesar is dead and Cleopatra has joined the Romans, so now he wants Cornelia as his promised reward. Ptolemy tells Achilla to go away; Achilla goes out grumpily, and so does Ptolemy, promising to return after he has dealt with his pesky sister. Cornelia and Sextus are distraught. He wants to kill himself (it runs in the family), but Cornelia tells him to buck up, and they scoot off to the Roman camp to join Cleopatra and try again to kill Ptolemy.

At the start of act 3, Achilla laments having been betrayed and tells us that he has changed sides. Not a good idea, as it turns out. A "battle symphony" ensues, one of those typical operatic things that gets it over with in about thirty seconds. This one also uses Handel's quick ending. The good guys lose. Ptolemy enters with Cleopatra as a hostage, singing a nasty aria about how much he hates her guts and how he's going to enjoy humiliating her. All this and sibling rivalry, too. Alone and under guard, Cleopatra laments her fate in one of the most famous arias that Handel ever wrote: "Piangerò la sorte mia:"

A
I shall weep at my fate, so cruel and terrible,
As long as I have life in my breast.

B
But when I die, wherever he may be,
My ghost will torment the tyrant day and night.

Actually, the famous part of this aria is its "A" section, and here we see the beauty of ABA form as a force for character development. The "B" section is a fast, vicious explosion of wrath which comes suddenly and from the depths of her soul. We have already heard Cleopatra feeling sorry for herself in her previous aria. Now, she will cry, but also have her revenge even if it comes from beyond the grave. She may be bowed, but she's not broken. This aria has no ritornello at all; it begins with the voice right away, yet another example of Handel's concern to keep things moving even at slow tempos.

Next, Caesar has his big scene. It takes place by the side of the harbor near Alexandria, the site of the earlier battle. Handel writes an extensive prelude, evocative of the gentle breezes mentioned in the upcoming aria. This introduces Caesar's accompanied recitative, followed by his consoling "Aure, deh, per pietà" ("Oh, you breezes, have pity"). As before, with "V'adoro pupille," the thematic unity between the orchestral introductions and the actual arias creates a larger musical unit, opening out the traditional ABA form and lending the music a stronger feeling of continuity. Here, the "B" section is another accompagnato, harking back to the one preceding the aria. So, although this is technically a da capo aria, the form comes across as ABABA, with all of the repeats being variations of the original idea, and playing for about twelve minutes.

Sextus then enters with the dying Achilla, who was mortally wounded in that evening's battle. Caesar hides. Achilla tells Sextus that a hundred men are waiting to do battle and will follow whoever bears the royal seal. This he gives to Sextus, along with the whereabouts of a secret passage into the palace, and then he dies. Caesar reveals himself to Sextus who, shocked, asks Caesar how he survived. "I swam," he replies. Together they dash off to round up the troops and rescue Cleopatra, who is in the palace bidding a last farewell to her handmaidens. Her second accompanied recitative really comprises an independent number lasting some two and half minutes:

> Accompagnato:
> You, who were once my faithful handmaidens,
> Cry in vain; you are mine no longer.
> My barbaric brother, who has stolen the crown from me,
> Has taken you away from me, just as he will shortly take my life.
> [*noises off*]
> But what is this noise of battle?
> Ah yes, you are mine no longer;
> You will see Cleopatra's soul expire.

Enter Caesar with troops. The two lovers celebrate a brief reunion. Caesar tells Cleopatra that he is off to renew the battle against Ptolemy, and that she should meet him at the harbor. She agrees, but not before singing "Da tempeste il legno infranto," that sailor's hornpipe that we heard way back at the beginning of this book:

> A
> When the storm-damaged ship safely arrives into port,
> It no longer knows what it desires.
>
> B
> So the heart, after pain and sorrow and once it has found comfort,
> Returns the soul to joy.

Musically this piece may remind you of Cleopatra's first aria, but while the carefree exuberance may be similar, there are significant differences. This music sounds stronger, sturdier, and less frivolous. It has grown up. This is also the only aria that Cleopatra sings that isn't directly about herself—how pretty, smart, sexy, deserving, miserable, or sad she feels at any particular moment. Rather, it describes what can only be called a life lesson. The logic may be dicey, or maybe it's just my translation, but there is wisdom here, an attempt to describe the broader human condition.

So Cleopatra's experiences have changed her, and we realize this because we have had the chance to compare her expression of related moods. Some might say that creating a character involves showing as wide a range of different feelings as possible, and that is true up to a point. But creating a *realistic* character requires personalizing those feelings, adding nuance, and that means visiting some of them multiple times. This takes compositional genius, obviously, but at an even more basic level it takes time. One of Handel greatest gifts, and it really is one of the very greatest, is the ability to write long without writing dull. It's not something a composer can learn; it's an instinctive quality.

The rest of the opera is wrap-up. Ptolemy, unaware of what has been happening, tries to force himself on Cornelia. Tired of all of the failed assassination attempts and determined to finish the job herself, she comes at him with a dagger. Not to be outdone by his mother, Sextus bursts in and, after a brief—really brief—like five seconds of secco recitative brief—fight, he runs Ptolemy through with his sword. Cornelia sings about it for a bit, then everyone gathers at the harbor for the final celebration. Caesar and Cleopatra get a jubilant duet, which we need not quote, and the whole cast and chorus joins in to praise joy, peace and love.

The opportunity to savor character development constitutes the major argument in favor of listening to complete works, as opposed to excerpts or aria recitals. This is the main "something extra" that extended listening affords. The example on disc that proves this rule is Natalie Dessay's marvelous program for Erato called *Cleopatra*, mentioned briefly in the previous chapter. This recital contains all of the Egyptian queen's music from the opera, more or less. Two arias are missing: Cleopatra's initial entrance, "Non disperar; chi sà?" and her third aria, "Tu la mia stella sei." Instead, we get the stern "Per dar vita all'idol mio," never used, and whose music was transferred to Sextus later on in the opera, and a very beautiful siciliano "Troppo crudeli siete," which Handel ultimately replaced with "Piangerò la sorte mia."

While it's lovely to have the opportunity to hear some of Handel's alternative thoughts on the role, removing two of Cleopatra's "fluffier" early arias eliminates some of the nuance that contributes to her authenticity as a character. On the other hand, it does heighten her seriousness sooner than required on stage. Dramatically speaking, it would have been impossible to have "Troppo crudeli" and "Piangerò," both long, (initially) slow, and of similar intent, follow one another in quick succession. It has to be one or the other, and it's easy to understand why Handel preferred the wild mood swings of the latter in contrast to the steady siciliano rhythms of the former. "Piangerò" says so much more about Cleopatra's personal combination of vulnerability and strength, but there's no reason we can't hear both pieces on an aria recital disc.

Cleopatra's story doesn't quite end here, however. She also appears as the female lead in the oratorio *Alexander Balus*. Ptolemy turns up again too, still a villain. Actually, it's not the same Cleopatra and Ptolemy, because the action in *Balus* takes place about a century and a half before that of *Giulio Cesare*; but they didn't call the Ptolemys a dynasty for nothing, and apparently lots of them had the same names. In any case, Handel seems to have had some interestingly similar views of his Cleopatras, worth taking a moment to explore.

For example, the oratorio Cleopatra gets a number—"Hark! He strikes the golden lyre"—scored for "exotic" instruments, in this case harp and mandolin, designed to showcase her feminine allure. Unlike "V'adoro pupille," though, where the intent is pure seduction, this Cleopatra shows up more as an Egyptian party planner. However, she quickly settles down and falls in love with Alexander, whom she marries. From then on she plays the part of the faithful wife. So the story is quite different, all the more so because it ends tragically, and yet Handel does all that he can to build a sympathetic character around a sequence of memorable arias and ensembles.

In particular, at the end of the oratorio, she has a cluster of extremely moving accompagnatos and arias that literally steal the show: "Shall Cleopatra ever smile again," "O take me from this hateful light," and lastly, "Convey me to some peaceful shore." In her circumstances and her music, she recalls another of Handel's major portraits of ladies in mourning who we already have met: Galatea; and like her later historical counterpart in *Giulio Cesare*, this Cleopatra's character grows and deepens over the course of the work, gaining in stature as she responds to the events of her marriage, her kidnapping by Ptolemy's "ruffians," and the loss of her husband.

Handel's Cleopatras, both of them really, refute the principal complaint leveled against baroque opera over the ensuing centuries—that contrived plots and unbending formal procedures prevent the sort of character development and sympathetic audience involvement that we find in, say, Wagner, Puccini, and Verdi. As I hope this and the previous chapter have shown, nothing could be further from the truth. All opera is inherently artificial, but its forms and conventions are tools that, properly used, and placed in the hands of a composer of genius, produce characters as vivid and real as the stage allows. Virtually every major Handel dramatic work will contain at least one such role—often more. As a composer for the theater, it was one of his major concerns, and a task at which he seldom if ever failed.

A Lotta Cantatas and Serenatas

Early Italian Pieces, Sacred Music, and English Ceremonial Works

I f the title of this chapter suggests to you a miscellaneous and somewhat random assortment of unrelated works, you'd be right. We have reached the bottom of our Handelian "food pyramid," in which resides a massive pile of great music—only a fraction of which we have room to discuss. Some of it is well known, but most of it is not. Fortunately, a great many of Handel's early and hitherto unknown pieces have been recorded, and we have every reason to expect more in the future. This chapter, then, surveys briefly and selectively, in roughly chronological order, a very large repertoire of music worth your consideration, beginning with:

Early Italian Instrumental Cantatas and Serenatas

■ *Ah! crudel, nel pianto mio* (HWV 79)
Scoring: soprano, 2 oboes, 2 violins, viola, and bass.[11]
Form:12 sonata (overture), 3 arias, 1 accompagnato.

■ *Alla caccia (Diana cacciatrice)* (HWV 79)
Scoring: soprano, soprano chorus, trumpet, 2 violins, and bass.
Form: march, 1 aria, 1 echo chorus.

■ *Alpestre monte* (HWV 81)
Scoring: soprano, 2 violins and bass.
Form: accompagnato, 2 arias.

Amarilli vezzosa (*Il duello amoroso*) (HWV 82)
Scoring: soprano, alto, 2 violins and bass.
Form: sonata, 4 arias, 1 duet (Aria a 2).

Arresta il passo (*Aminta e Fillide*) (HWV 83)
Scoring: 2 sopranos, 3 violins, viola, and bass.
Form: overture, 10 arias, 1 duet.

Cecilia, volgi un sguardo (HWV 89)
Scoring: soprano, tenor, 2 violins, viola, and bass.
Form: 3 arias, 1 duet.

Clori, mia bella Clori (HWV 92)
Scoring: soprano, 2 violins, and bass.
Form: 4 arias.

Cor fedele, in vano speri (*Clori, Tirsi e Fileno*) (HWV 96)
Scoring: 2 sopranos, alto, 2 flutes, 2 oboes, solo violin, 2 violins, 2
violas, archlute, and bass.
Form: overture, 12 arias, 2 duets, 1 trio.

Crudel tirano Amor (HWV 97)
Scoring: soprano, 2 oboes, 2 violins, viola, and bass.
Form: 3 arias.

Cuopre tal volta il cielo (HWV 98)
Scoring: basso13, 2 violins and bass.
Form: 1 accompagnato, 2 arias.

Da quel giorno fatale (*Delirio amoroso*) (HWV 99)
Scoring: soprano, flauto dolce, oboe, solo violin, 3 violins, viola,
cello solo, and bass.
Form: sonata, 3 arias, entrée, 1 arietta.

Dietro l'orme fugaci (*Armida abbandonata*) (HWV 105)
Scoring: soprano, 2 violins, and bass.
Form: 2 accompagnatos, 3 arias.

Dunque sarà pur vero (*Agrippina condotta a morire*) HWV (110)
Scoring: soprano, 2 violins, and bass.
Form: 4 arias, 1 arioso.

Echeggiate, festeggiate, Numi eterni (HWV 119)
Scoring: 3 sopranos, alto, basso, flauto dolce, 2 oboes, 2 violins, viola, cello and bass.
Form: 9 arias, 1 duet, 1 accompagnato.

Figlio d'alte speranze (HWV 113)
Scoring: soprano, 2 violins and bass.
Form: sonata, 3 arias.

La terra è liberata (*Apollo e Dafne*) (HWV 122)
Scoring: soprano, basso, flute, 2 oboes, solo violin, 2 violins, viola, solo cello, and bass.
Form: 8 arias, 2 duets.

Languia de bocca lusinghiera (HWV 123)
Scoring: soprano, oboe, violin, and bass.
Form: 1 aria.

Look down, harmonious Saint (HWV 124)
Scoring: tenor, 2 violins, viola, and bass.
Form: 1 accompagnato, 1 aria (based on HWV 89)

Mi palpita il cor (HWV 132c)
Scoring: alto, flute, and bass.
Form: 1 arioso, 2 arias.

Nel dolce dell'oblio (*Pensieri notturni di Filli*) (HWM 134)
Scoring: soprano, flauto dolce, and bass.
Form: 2 arias.

No se emendará jamás (HWV 140—and yes, it's in Spanish)
Scoring: soprano, guitar, and bass (cello).
Form: 2 arias.

Notte placida e cheta (HWV 142)
Scoring: soprano, 2 violins and bass.
Form: 4 arias, 2 accompagnatos.

Oh, come chiare e belle (HWV 143)
Scoring: 2 sopranos, alto, trumpet, 2 solo violins, 2 violins, and bass.
Form: sonata, 9 arias, 1 chorus.

▪ *Qual ti riveggio (Ero e Leandro)* (HWV 150)
  Scoring: soprano, 2 oboes, violin solo, 2 violins, viola, cello solo, and bass.
  Form: 3 arias.

▪ *Spande ancor a mio dispetto* (HWV 165)
  Scoring: basso, 2 violins, and bass.
  Form: 2 arias.

▪ *Splenda l'alba in oriente* (HWV 166)
  Scoring: alto, 2 flauti dolci, oboe, 2 violins, viola, and bass.
  Form: 2 arias.

▪ *Tra le fiamme (Il consiglio)* (HWV 170)
  Scoring: soprano, 2 flauti dolci, oboe, 2 violins, viola da gamba, and bass.
  Form: 3 arias.

▪ *Tu fedel? tu costante?* (HWV 171)
  Scoring: soprano, 2 violins, and bass.
  Form: sonata, 4 arias.

▪ *Un'alma innamorata* (HWV 173)
  Scoring: soprano, 2 violins in unison, and bass.
  Form: 3 arias.

I hope that this list piques your interest. Handel composed twenty-eight cantatas with instrumental accompaniment, out of about a hundred in all. No one knows the exact number for sure; every now and then a new one still turns up. *Clori, Tirsi e Fileno*, for instance, only appeared complete in 1960. The rest are for solo voice and continuo, and only one of those, *La Lucrezia* (HWV145), has achieved anything like wider exposure, at least on disc. On the other hand, some of the instrumental cantatas are making their way into the consciousness of connoisseurs, even if they remain all but unknown to the wider public. We need to fix that. These are gems.

As you can see from the summaries of form listed with each work, the cantatas come in every possible shape and size, from simple songs to mini-operas. Later in the century, the solo cantata, in the hands of

Alessandro Scarlatti (Domenico's dad), became relatively standard-ized as a short piece containing two recitative/aria pairs, and some of Handel's do that as well, but there is no hard and fast rule. In these works he was demonstrating a newly acquired mastery of his craft. He enjoyed total freedom in creating them, writing with love and evident care for his Italian patrons, many of whom wrote the poems.

You will notice that some of the cantatas have two names. The first, invariably, consists of the first line of sung text; the second is simply a general title. Don't be confused if you see one and not the other. Both are correct, and they appear interchangeably in the literature and on disc. I tend to prefer the alternate titles because they usually are shorter and let you know at least what or who the thing's about.

Some of these cantatas have already been mentioned, including *Agrippina condotta a morire* in connection with the opera named after her, and *Aminta e Fillide* for the arias that Handel took from it and reused later. Indeed, Handel took arias, or bits of them, from all of these pieces and incorporated them into later works. They constitute his musical "savings account," and the fact he was still mining them decades later should be taken as the strongest possible indication of their high quality and musical value.

Although the instrumentation ranges from solo guitar or flute, to a few violins, to what is effectively a full orchestral complement, this really is vocal chamber music. Even if we are familiar with a particu-lar number from a later setting, there's a very special freshness and intimacy in hearing the original settings. For example, the aria "Ogni vento" from *Agrippina*, included on the sample disc, involves the full string orchestra with oboes in the opera. Scored for just two violin parts plus continuo in the cantata *Aminta e Fillide*, the music has a distinctive rhythmic clarity and bounce. Both are delightful; neither is inherently preferable.

You might feel that this is inconsistent with my general preference for Handel at his most lavish, and my consequent disdain for period instrument performances that present his works in miniature (usually, as I mentioned, for financial reasons dressed up as artistic ones). Any contradiction, however, is more apparent than real. I object to making Handel sound small when he plainly intended the opposite. Here, there is no question about what he wanted, and the only performance issue as regards instrumental forces in the cantatas is the need to have a few extra strings on hand now and then. The rest is self-evident.

Many of the cantatas involve characters that we have come to know. Armida, of *Rinaldo* fame, gets to vent her misery all over again in *Armida abbandonata*. The legendary story of Hero and Leander takes center stage in *Qual ti riveggio*. Always ripe for a musical setting, it even served as inspiration for a twentieth-century tone poem by Victor Herbert, no less. *Apollo e Dafne* tells the familiar tale of the god's pursuit of the nature-loving Daphne, and her subsequent transformation into a laurel tree. This myth also became an opera by Richard Strauss. The participants in *Echeggiate, festeggiate, Numi eterni* are all Roman gods and goddesses, while the fickle shepherdess Clori turns up on more than one occasion. *Clori, Tirsi e Fileno*, a pastoral comedy, is the longest of the instrumental cantatas. It has two parts, or acts, and it serves as a lighthearted counterpart in serenata form to *Aci, Galatea e Polifemo*.

When it comes to recordings, we are in good shape, but it's a very recent phenomenon. Several of the above works remain undocumented. Marco Vitale and his instrumental ensemble Contrasto Armonico have embarked on a complete cantata survey, and that will be a major undertaking if and when it is complete. There are about half a dozen issues at present, most featuring the excellent Roberta Mameli, split over two labels: Brilliant Classics and Ayros (Vitale's own imprint). Nearly all of the instrumental cantatas have been recorded for Glossa by La Risonanza under Fabio Bonizzoni, featuring another splendid Roberta—Invernizzi. This outstanding series, ten volumes so far, also includes a first rate version of *Aci, Galatea e Polifemo*, as well as the *Italian Duets and Trios* (scandalous source of a few numbers in *Messiah*) and the *Chamber Duets*.

There are also quite a few highly recommendable stand-alone productions, with more always coming. For a brief sample: Soprano Eva Mei joins Il Giardino Armonico on Teldec/Erato as three women scorned or abandoned (or both): Agrippina, Armida, and Lucrezia. Countertenor Andreas Scholl and soprano Hélène Guilmette lock horns in *Il duello amoroso* plus three other cantatas, including the delicious *Mi palpita il cor*, on Harmonia Mundi. The same label, with Nicholas McGegan conducting, couples *Clori, Tirsi e Fileno* with *Apollo e Dafne*, while Hyperion has an excellent version of *Aminta e Fillide* with Gillian Fisher, Patrizia Kwella, and the London Handel Orchestra under Denys Darlow.

Drawing an analogy to instrumental music, if Handel's operas and oratorios are his symphonies, then the cantatas are his string quartets. They make less noise than the works for larger forces, but they are no less approachable, entertaining, or expressive. If you love vocal music, you will discover here some of Handel's writing for the voice at its most subtle and exquisite. I find the fact that the instrumental cantatas represent merely the most visible portion of a vast, largely unexplored repertoire—the tip of a musical iceberg—very exciting. It means that there are still new discoveries waiting to be made, and we, as explorers, will have the opportunity to make them. For a music lover, what could be more fun than that?

Sacred Music

Latin Church Music

- Gloria in B-flat
- Dixit Dominus
- Nisi Dominus
- Salve Regina
- Saeviat tellus inter rigores
- Laudate pueri Dominum
- Silete venti

The situation with Handel's sacred music is complicated, as I mentioned earlier, by the fact that there was no market for his Catholic liturgical works after he left Italy, and most of his English pieces are inextricably involved with his contributions to various royal ceremonies and special occasions. They properly belong in a separate category of their own—the ceremonial music—that we will touch on below. Exactly how much Handel may have written while in Italy (and before), whom he wrote it for, and exactly when, often remains a mystery.

Adding to the uncertainty, you may see recordings or concerts announcing something called Handel's *Roman Vespers* or *Carmelite Vespers*. Let the buyer beware. There is no such thing. Certain scholar/ performers have conjectured that Handel's Latin church music may have been intended for a specific liturgy, and so they have taken it upon themselves to reconstruct an entire service around the various pieces. This means filling out the bits that Handel didn't write with music by other composers, Gregorian chant, and other stuff, none of which has anything to do with the point of the entire operation, namely, enjoying Handel's Latin liturgical music.

Don't get me wrong: there are some great Vespers settings out there—Monteverdi's for instance—but that setting enjoys the singular advantage of having been entirely written by the composer in question. So don't get snookered into thinking you will discover a new, large work of Handel, when in truth what is really being offered is an assortment of the above works, organized as they might have been in an actual service. That means giving little or no consideration to finding the best and most enjoyable order for continuous listening, never mind all of the musical roughage that takes up the space between Handel's contributions.

One big discovery in recent decades has been the charming and vivacious Gloria for soprano and strings. It was authenticated in 2001 on the basis of its relationship to later works—always a good bet with Handel, assuming he wasn't simply borrowing from someone else. Although the actual date of composition remains unknown, it has been suggested that the work comes from Handel's late Hamburg period, shortly before he left for Italy. It's a multimovement setting that plays for about fifteen minutes, and it has been recorded a few times—most notably by John Eliot Gardiner with soprano Gillian Keith for Decca.

The forms of Christian liturgical music can be very difficult to keep straight. The meanings of the same terms have changed over the centuries to suit the needs of the various denominations and their unique liturgies, resulting in a virtually useless terminological jumble. For example, run a Google search and you'll find this definition of "motet" from Britania.com: "Typically, it is a Latin religious choral composition, yet it can be a secular composition or a work for soloist(s) and instrumental accompaniment, in any language, with or without a choir."

Isn't that helpful? In order to make life easier, I offer the following three categories into which just about all Christian liturgical music falls:

1. Settings of the standard five-part Mass (called the "Ordinary"), or one of its sections
2. Psalm settings, usually identified by name and also sometimes called motets, anthems, canticles, or something else entirely
3. Other well-known prayers, such as the Te Deum, Stabat Mater, Magnificat, Requiem, and Salve Regina, or anything else based on a biblical or freely written religious text that may form part of a service. These too might be called a hymn, anthem, motet, antiphon, canticle—you name it, and it doesn't really matter which. For example, the Utrecht Te Deum is listed in the HWV catalogue as a canticle, but the Jubilate that comes with it, also listed as a canticle, later became an anthem: specifically, the First Chandos Anthem. And this, despite the fact that it is also a psalm—Psalm 100, to be exact. So just take them as they come.

Handel's Latin liturgical music includes all of the above. The Gloria is one of the principal sections of the Mass. Dixit Dominus, Nisi Dominus, and Laudate pueri Dominum are all psalms. The other works fall into the category of solo motet, a form basically identical to that of the contemporaneous instrumental cantata—that is, a sequence of recitatives and arias for a single soloist. All of these pieces are special in one way or another, thanks to Handel's unfailingly vivid response to the texts. The three psalm settings are the largest in scale due to the participation of the chorus. Let's see how Handel organizes each one musically.

Nisi Dominus (Psalm 127/126)

1. Except the Lord build the house, they labour in vain that build it: except the Lord keep the city, the watchman waketh but in vain. [chorus]
2. It is vain for you to rise up early, to sit up late, to eat the bread of sorrows: [tenor solo]
3. for so he giveth his beloved sleep. Lo, children are an heritage of the Lord: and the fruit of the womb is his reward. [alto solo]

4. As arrows are in the hand of a mighty man; so are children of the youth. [bass solo]

5. Happy is the man that hath his quiver full of them: they shall not be ashamed, but they shall speak with the enemies in the gate. [tenor solo]

[6. Glory be to the Father, to the Son, and to the Holy Spirit, as it was in the beginning, as it is now, and as it shall be forever, world without end, amen.] [chorus]

This is the lightest of Handel's three major psalm settings. The arrangement of the text does not follow the verse structure of the original psalm; rather, Handel has organized the words to fit his musical forces: alto, tenor, and bass soloists and choir, creating a balanced musical structure. The concluding line, "Glory be to the Father, etc.," called the "doxology," is not part of the psalm; it is, rather, a formula traditionally used to conclude the prayer. It offers an excellent musical opportunity to write a large, usually contrapuntal conclusion, while the words, "as it was in the beginning" provide a good excuse to bring back the music of the opening, which Handel, and just about every other composer with any sense, does.

The opening chorus has an accompaniment that sounds amazingly like a sort of puppy-dog version of *Zadok the Priest*—it's smaller, friskier, and absolutely adorable. Handel uses his patented fast ending to close this number, showing us just how early this stylistic trait became typical. The solos then follow symmetrically, the tenor's two numbers framing the alto and bass, each singing a tiny aria lasting between a minute and a half and two minutes, before a grand double chorus wraps up the whole business. A brief reference to the opening ushers in the joyous conclusion. Playing for about twelve minutes, the piece has become relatively popular on disc, with a particularly fine version available on Chandos from Harry Christophers and The Sixteen (coupled to the Dixit Dominus and Silete venti).

Laudate pueri Dominum (Psalm 113/112)

1. Praise ye the Lord. Praise, O ye servants of the Lord, praise the name of the Lord. [solo with chorus]

2. Blessed be the name of the Lord from this time forth and for evermore. [solo with oboe]
3. From the rising of the sun unto the going down of the same the Lord's name is to be praised. [solo with chorus]
4. The Lord is high above all nations, and his glory above the heavens. [solo with 2 oboes]
5. Who is like unto the Lord our God, who dwelleth on high, who humbleth himself to behold the things that are in heaven, and in the earth! [chorus]
6. He raiseth up the poor out of the dust, and lifteth the needy out of the dunghill; that he may set him with princes, even with the princes of his people. [solo plus continuo]
7. He maketh the barren woman to keep house, and to be a joyful mother of children. Praise ye the Lord. [solo with violins]
[8. Glory be to the Father, to the Son, and to the Holy Spirit, as it was in the beginning, as it is now, and as it shall be forever, world without end, amen.] [solo with chorus]

The celebratory tone of this psalm suggests to Handel some of those massive choral effects that he always used so effectively, and which will return in his ceremonial works and the big oratorios to come. There is only one soloist, a mezzo-soprano, who joins in the opening and closing choruses. These are not fugues, but massive, concerto-like alternations of solo flourishes with thrilling, block harmonies. In between, solo arias alternate with powerful choral statements. Scored for strings with two oboes, the woodwinds get a major workout in the soprano's two arias, Nos. 2 and 4, with the major contrapuntal movement for the chorus falling in between.

In Nisi Dominus, the reference back to the opening occurs at the start of the final "Gloria Patri" chorus. Here Handel does just the opposite. Initially, the chorus dances away with the soloist in a lilting triple meter (3/8). Suddenly, at the words "as it was in the beginning," the time signature switches to that of the first movement (4/4) and we do indeed return to the beginning, with the soprano's brilliant coloratura atop the rich chords in the chorus and strings. Divided violas add additional resonance to the string textures at the choral climaxes, and as you can see from the outline of the scoring, Handel creates as much color and textural variety as possible in his scoring of the solo numbers.

For reasons that elude me completely, the Laudate pueri Dominum[14] remains a rarity on recordings. Musically it's as good as any of its companions, and it plays for only a bit more than a quarter hour. The best version, without a doubt, is Minkowski's on Archiv, with Magdalena Kožená a first-rate soloist. That disc also includes Dixit Dominus, the Salve Regina, and the motet Saeviat tellus. It's impossible to get all of Handel's Latin church music without some duplication unless you opt for digital downloads. That way you can select only what you need, and for many listeners this may be the best option.

Finally, here's an intriguing fun fact that may give some clue as to how Handel's mind worked. He reused a lot of the Laudate pueri in the oratorio *Joshua*, but the work's seventh movement, about making housewives out of barren women and giving them children, became the Second Harlot's aria "They sentence, great King, is prudent and wise," in *Solomon*. Coincidence? Compassion for an otherwise wicked character? Ironic commentary? Make of that what you will.

Dixit Dominus (Psalm 110/109)

1. The Lord said unto my Lord, Sit thou at my right hand, until I make thine enemies thy footstool. [chorus with soloists]
2. The Lord shall send the rod of thy strength out of Zion: rule thou in the midst of thine enemies. [alto solo with continuo]
3. Thy people shall be willing in the day of thy power, in the beauties of holiness from the womb of the morning: thou hast the dew of thy youth. [soprano solo with strings]
4. The Lord hath sworn, and will not repent. [chorus]
5. Thou art a priest for ever after the order of Melchizedek. [chorus]
6. The Lord at thy right hand shall strike through kings in the day of his wrath. [chorus with soloists]
7. He shall judge among the heathen, he shall fill the places with the dead bodies; he shall wound the heads over many countries. [chorus]
8. He shall drink of the brook in the way: therefore shall he lift up the head. [2 solo sopranos plus choral tenors and basses]

[9. Glory be to the Father, to the Son, and to the Holy Spirit, as it was in the beginning, as it is now, and as it shall be forever, world without end, amen.] [chorus]

Dixit Dominus is Laudate pueri's evil twin. If the latter represents light and joy, then the former offers a dramatic portrayal of death and destruction. This of course explains its ongoing popularity. We have already considered in the introduction the extract included on the accompanying disc, and that is also certainly one of the best complete recordings to own, along with the Minkowski just mentioned, or possibly one of John Eliot Gardiner's two versions (for Erato or Decca). In any event, the work is very well served in the current discography, and comes coupled every which way, both with other works of Handel as well as those by other composers. Take your pick.

This piece has been described by various authorities, quite aptly, as a concerto for voices and orchestra. There are five soloists (two sopranos, alto, tenor, and bass), a five-part choir (same), and a five-part string section (2 violins, 2 violas, and bass). Handel arranges these forces much like a concerto grosso, with the solos often deployed as a unit against the larger forces. The result has a remarkably fluid density of texture, which in turn helps to give the music its characteristic intensity of expression. There's nothing quite like the effect achieved when the massed voices of the chorus yield to the personalized timbre of the soloists (and vice versa) in the same music. Handel exploits the contrast masterfully, and takes great care not to lessen the impact by overdoing it.

He also took tremendous pains over his notation. At two points in the fourth movement, Handel actually writes in a gradual decrescendo. Since the word didn't yet exist (as a musical term at least), he writes it out: piano, then pianissimo, then pianississimo. This is just another of many extraordinary passages in a work that makes huge demands on its performers, to the delight of its listeners. Playing for between thirty to thirty-five minutes in most performances, this is both Handel's largest psalm setting as well as his greatest.

Having spent some time with the three psalms we can consider the motets more briefly. They certainly are no less worthy, and are very

different from each other. The least known is Saeviat tellus inter rigores, for the simple reason that the name is unpronounceable as well as
forgettable, and the words comprise a sort of pep rally in support of the
order of Carmelite nuns. Now, I won't go so far as to say that no one
cares about the Carmelites. Poulenc, after all, wrote a devastating opera
called *Dialogues of the Carmelites* in which an entire convent submits to
martyrdom during the French Revolution. Let's just say that Carmelite
devotional poetry remains a subject for specialized tastes.

The music, on the other hand, is another story altogether. Handel
had a knack, whenever he had a great text, of coming up with settings
redolent of every telling word and image. When the poem wasn't so
special, on the other hand, he just wrote thrilling music and elevated
the words to the level of the composition. This is what happens here.
Scored for oboes and strings, the soprano's initial aria shares many
stylistic traits, including its sheer virtuoso abandon, with "Disseratevi"
from *La Resurrezione*, and that's saying a lot. The slow movement, "O
nox dulcis," is purely gorgeous, and the concluding "Alleluia" is one of
the most dizzyingly insane pieces ever conceived for the soprano voice.
You might call it the musical equivalent of an Olympic figure skater's
final spin—only lasting about two minutes. You can hear the piece on
the Minkowski disc mentioned above, fearlessly sung by soprano Annick
Massis, or by the death-defying Julia Lezhneva, with works by Vivaldi,
Porpora, and Mozart, on her Decca debut album.

The Salve Regina ("Hail, Queen") is a prayer for the intercession of
the Virgin Mary (and the last prayer in the Rosary). It was set about a
trillion times in the baroque period. I've heard only one or two million
of them, but most tend to stress the graceful, sweet, lyrical, feminine
side of the subject. Handel is positively expressionistic in comparison.
He seems to have noticed the lines "To you we cry, the banished children of Eve; and to you we sigh, mourning and crying in this vale of
tears." At the word "sigh" ("suspiramus"), Handel has the singer almost
suffocating, barely able to utter a sound. Sure, the music recovers in
cheerful hope of Mary's intercession (with a warbling organ solo), but
he sets the final plea as an accompagnato, *adagissimo* (basically, "as slow
as humanly possible"), and pianissimo, in a gesture of utter abasement.
This is not your mom's average Salve Regina.

Silete venti actually dates from the 1720s, well after Handel's Italian apprenticeship. It may have been written in or for Italy, however, as Handel traveled there periodically to recruit singers for his opera company in London. The title means "Be silent, winds," the text being an original poem expressing the soul's joy in uniting with Jesus. The words are full of the sort of nature imagery that Handel loved to express in music, while the opening is a huge overture more than six minutes long whose rushing strings are interrupted by the soprano's first words—a brilliant theatrical stroke similar to that at the start of *Aminta e Fillide*.

This is a substantial piece that lasts a bit over twenty-five minutes in performance. There have always been good recordings available including Lynne Dawson's on Chandos, or Karina Gauvin's on Dorian/Sono Luminus. Noted Dutch soprano and lieder specialist Elly Ameling made a lovely version for Philips (now Decca) that hopefully will see the light of day again soon. It's tempting to say, in summary, that Handel's Latin sacred music makes up for in quality what it lacks in quantity—if only his later work did not possess an abundance of both.

Chandos Anthems

1. *O be joyful in the Lord*
2. *In the Lord put I my trust*
3. *Have mercy upon me*
4. *O sing unto the Lord a new song*
5. *I will magnify thee*
6. *As pants the hart for cooling streams*
7. *My song shall be alway* [Note: not "always"]
8. *O come, let us sing unto the Lord*
9. *O praise the Lord with one consent*
10. *The Lord is my light*
11. *Let God arise*
[12. Chandos Te Deum in B-flat]

Handel composed his Chandos Anthems in 1717–18. All of them are psalm settings or paraphrases. The Te Deum is not, strictly speaking, one of the anthems, but it usually gets mentioned in the same breath. Aside from being his major efforts at sacred music in English, and lovely pieces in their own right, the Anthems have a fascinating relationships with both earlier and later music, as we've already seen. The reason for this has a lot to do with the special circumstances of their composition.

It has always been very expensive to keep a private musical establishment, and even the very wealthy in Handel's day found it a strain. Handel's orchestra at Cannons, the country estate of the Duke of Chandos, had no violas and his choir lacked altos, at least initially. The first six anthems require a three part chorus, very unusual at the time, while the remainder employ the more usual four or five parts. Orchestrally, aside from the missing violas, Handel had an oboe, a bassoon, and a couple of recorders in Nos. 8 and 10. He wrote the original versions of *Acis and Galatea* and *Esther* for this same musical establishment (which is why they aren't performed that way today, and weren't after Handel left the duke's employ).

Rather than serving as a limitation, these restrictions seem to have stimulated Handel's imagination. In some cases, such as Anthem No. 1, he arranged existing music (the Utrecht Jubilate and Laudate pueri) for his smaller forces without any loss of musical substance. The early oratorios, on the other hand, drew on and expanded some of the anthems liberally. For the Chapel Royal, Handel shortened and otherwise adapted several pieces, so some exist in multiple versions, including the Chandos Te Deum, *I will magnify thee*, and *Let God arise*. He made at least five settings of *As pants the hart* for various occasions.

In short, with the Chandos Anthems—like the early cantatas— Handel created a reservoir of music to be savored for its own sake, and used in the future. They are not essential acquisitions for your basic Handel collection, but wonderful to get to know once you've become familiar with the major works in their immediate proximity. They have not been frequently recorded, but what exists, fortunately, is excellent. The Chandos recording of all eleven anthems, featuring The Sixteen under Harry Christophers, is the reference edition, and there are also two fine discs on Hyperion, directed by Stephen Layton. The Chandos Te Deum hasn't gotten much attention outside of biographies and other specialized literature. After all, Handel wrote at least five Te Deum settings—surely too much of a good thing.

Ceremonial Music

- *Ode for the Birthday of Queen Anne* (1713)
- Utrecht Te Deum and *Jubilate* (1713)
- Caroline Te Deum (1714)
- Four Coronation Anthems (1727)
- *Zadok the Priest*
- *Let Thy Hand Be Strengthened*
- *The King Shall Rejoice*
- *My Hears Is Inditing*
- Funeral Anthem for Queen Caroline (1737)
- Dettingen Te Deum and Anthem (1743)
- Foundling Hospital Anthem (1749)

These are the ceremonial works that made Handel an English musical icon in his own lifetime. There is more than a little irony in this fact. The reason Handel had the opportunity to compose most of them is because he was German and the English court also was German, freshly arrived from Hanover and not terribly popular. The choice of Handel as composer for major public events, then, was not without political controversy. Save for the years 1723–27, when he finally became a British citizen, he was never formally in service to the Chapel Royal. That position went to native composers, such as William Croft and Maurice Greene, true Anglicans familiar with the daily religious rituals of the court. Handel, on the other hand, was "of counsel," as they say in the legal profession: associated with the firm, but not officially a partner.

Still formally employed by the House of Hanover in 1713, Handel had been spending most of the past several years in London. The premiere of *Rinaldo* in 1711 had made him the hottest composer in town, and he enjoyed good relations with members of the royal establishment. In short, he was in demand. As already mentioned in connection with the track "Eternal source of light divine," the *Ode for the Birthday of Queen Anne* may or may not have been performed for its dedicatee, but when the commission came to compose the Utrecht Te Deum later that year, Handel was ready, willing and able.

Although the name of the prayer is always given in Latin, the words were set in English. The piece really needs a better title. "Te Deum" just means "You God," which is rather silly, but that's the tradition. The long form "Te Deum laudamus," or "We praise You God" is much better—at least it makes sense. Handel's setting caused a sensation, blowing away all previous Te Deums (and there were quite a few). Scored for pairs of trumpets and oboes, flute, strings, and a chorus of up to seven parts plus solos that come and go (much as in *Dixit Dominus*), the music is both heartfelt and grand. It lasts a bit more than twenty minutes, and the only reason we don't hear more of it is because Handel later outdid himself with the Dettingen Te Deum of 1743.

Handel added the Jubilate, a setting of Psalm 100 (99 in the Vulgate), shortly after writing the main item. It draws on the Laudate pueri at the start, but soon goes its own way. Shorter than the Te Deum by about five minutes, the two together would make a very rewarding first half of a modern choral concert, and no doubt proved just as satisfying in Handel's own day. There's a very handy recording of the pair on Channel Classics, with the Netherlands Bach Society led by Jos van Veldhoven. The program has a very appealing bonus, the *Ode for the Peace of Utrecht* by Handel's rival and contemporary William Croft. It's well worth hearing, and it proves quite decisively that Handel wasn't the only show in town.

Having ingratiated himself both to the public and the powers that be, Handel was in the best possible position when his somewhat grumpy employer became the king of England in 1714. The Caroline Te Deum may in fact have been composed for George I's arrival in the British capital, but Handel (and everyone else) liked the then princess of Wales, later queen, much better, and she in turn supported him. So, she got the Te Deum. It's what you'd expect for the occasion: peppy, brash, and short, with plenty of work for the trumpets and a few quieter solo numbers to give the ear a rest. Not a masterpiece, perhaps, but good clean fun.

Handel expressed his affection for Queen Caroline in a far more telling manner when she died in 1737. The funeral anthem that he composed is a deeply moving piece written with the utmost conviction. Scored only for chorus with two oboes, strings, and continuo, the music is actually highly varied and sustains its forty-five minutes unexpectedly well. As a sincere public expression of mourning it was very successful; as the first part of *Israel in Egypt* it bombed, and it has led a separate life ever since. Seldom performed and clearly a connoisseur's piece, it has received a surprising number of recordings, both in tandem with the oratorio and independently. I mean, it's not as if many listeners come home from a hard day's work and say, "Hmm. I feel like playing Queen Caroline's funeral anthem this evening." Then again, you never know. William Christie has made a splendid recording of the both the Caroline Te Deum and the Funeral Anthem for his own label, Les Arts Florissants Editions. That is the way to go.

We have already touched on the Coronation Anthems in chapter 1, but I include them here again for two reasons. First, they were the pieces that built on the reputation that Handel earned in writing the Utrecht Te Deum and made him *the* English ceremonial composer. Second, you can see from their date (1727) that Handel's major appearances for state occasions seem to have been relatively evenly spaced throughout his career—about once per decade or so. This kept him in the public eye at regular intervals with works designed to appeal to more than just opera-goers or paying attendees at the theater.

By the time Handel came to write the Dettingen Te Deum in 1743, he was in competition with no one but himself. The new work is twice as long as the Utrecht Te Deum. It has even more trumpets, plus timpani, three independent soloists (alto, tenor, bass), and a five-part chorus throughout. It is the grandest setting of the text that anyone cares about before Berlioz, a century later. This music came to represent Handel's public voice in the years immediately following his death, featuring prominently on such occasions as the twenty-fifth-anniversary celebrations in 1784. Sung and played over the years by monstrous choirs and orchestras, subtlety may not be the work's strong point, but there's really nothing like it as an exuberant expression of public celebration.

The anthem that Handel composed to go along with the Te Deum may come as a surprise: *The King Shall Rejoice.* No, this is not another version of the Coronation Anthem of the same title. The music is completely different, and after the first line, so is the text. This hasn't stopped it from being almost totally neglected, both in concert and on disc. Granted Handel filched some music from *Semele* for one of the choruses, but that doesn't explain it. Perhaps the overwhelming popularity of the earlier anthem leaves no room for any competition. In any case, there is only one outstanding recording that gives you the complete "Dettingen experience:" Trevor Pinnock's on Archiv. However, there are many fine versions of the Te Deum alone, most notably Stephen Layton's for Hyperion. That one comes with an organ concerto and a killer, slam-bang version of *Zadok the Priest*.

In the Foundling Hospital Anthem, Handel banked on his reputation to support a charity particularly close to his heart. It is a musical gesture of kindness, generosity, and compassion. The text speaks of the virtue of helping the poor and needy, but the work's great claim to fame resides in the fact that it concludes with the "Hallelujah Chorus." It's important to keep in mind that *Messiah* was not a success at its initial London performances. It took some time to catch on, so it only made sense for Handel to reuse its most famous chorus in another worthy context. After *Messiah*'s enduring fame was no longer an issue, Handel donated a set of parts to the Foundling Hospital for charitable use and the Anthem vanished from the repertoire. It has been nicely recorded several times, though, by Simon Preston for L'Oiseau-Lyre, and by David Hill with the Choir of Winchester Cathedral on Decca, among others.

Handel's ceremonial works, with the exception of the Dettingen Te Deum and the Coronation Anthems, have not worn so well over the years despite the acclaim they originally brought him. The Te Deum remains popular, the carping of the critics notwithstanding, while the Anthems basically lie beyond any criticism at all. I mean, could anything be more pointless? That said, it's not Handel's fault if we can't get too excited about the Peace of Utrecht, or the death of Queen Caroline, and no one should have to run out and buy five Te Deums by the same composer. Even if these aren't Handel's greatest or most collectable pieces, they still get the job done in an entertaining and often brilliant way.

It seems to me that what matters most is not that we fail to find these ceremonial pieces as compelling as Handel's audiences did, but rather that his genius was so all-encompassing that every generation can listen to whatever it likes, and have so much fun in the process. The value in trying to see him whole is not to say that we must accept everything equally and indiscriminately, but rather to help us pick and choose, from the most advantageous perspective, whatever gives us the most pleasure. Today, when it's practically impossible to find anyone who does not know the "Hallelujah Chorus," it's useful to remember that there was a time when Handel had to think hard about finding someplace else to put it, even as everyone was humming "Lascia ch'io pianga."

Secondhand Handel
Borrowing and Musical Morality

Handel's happy habit of borrowing and adapting musical ideas, heck, even entire movements, from himself as well as just about everyone he encountered, dead or alive, remains a subject of tremendous controversy. Publications of scholarly editions of Handel's sources purport to reveal the names of those whose work the dastardly composer pilfered for his own money-grubbing purposes, and his practice of self-borrowing has been noted frequently in previous chapters. Victorian writers, in particular, had a difficult time justifying the practice on moral grounds, especially when a favorite chestnut of sacred music turned out to come from a very secular source.

Interestingly, virtually all of Handel's opera librettos were adapted without permission from earlier ones that in turn derived from published plays and poems. What is curious about this generally known and accepted fact is that in all of the Handel literature, and all of the discussion about musical borrowings and adaptations, you will almost never see anyone who has moral or aesthetic qualms regarding the sourcing of his texts. I mean, if anything was just plain stolen, then they were. The reason that no one especially cares must stem from the fact that most assume that opera librettos and the like are common coin and have no artistic value, but that really isn't the point. Theft is theft. Of course, musicologists are mostly concerned with music, and rightly so, but the double standard is worth noting nonetheless.

Handel's apologists (of which I am one) point to two arguments in his favor. First, if in Handel's day everyone borrowed and no one gets terribly worked up about it when it comes to discussions of other composers, why is he singled out? Bach, for example, borrowed from

Handel and history hasn't shamed him for it. Then again, not all composers are English national icons. No one wants an icon who also happens to be a major plagiarist. Second, whatever Handel did by way of
revision or alteration to something he snatched from elsewhere—and
he never left anything entirely alone—arguably represents a distinct
and audible improvement. In other words, strictly musically, the ends
justifies the means.

Handel's Hamburg friend Johann Mattheson (1681–1764), one of
the great musical authorities of the period, stated very clearly that borrowing was acceptable as long as composers returned the borrowing
with interest—that is, they enriched and beautified whatever they borrowed. However, this is only one aspect of a bigger picture that often
gets downplayed in discussing this question, and that is the relationship between the performer and the musical text. Artists in Handel's
day reserved the right to alter a work virtually at will, well beyond
matters of mere ornamentation of the melodic line. A large piece,
such as an opera, needed to be adapted to every new cast and adjusted
to meet local taste, and it was the job of the local music director or
Kappellmeister to make the necessary revisions.

In other words, faithfulness to the work's original conception was
unheard of, even if the person doing the altering was the actual composer. Handel had no scruples about mangling his own music to ensure
the success of a specific performance. Everything was subject to circum-
stance. If a famous singer showed up with a few surefire, ready-made
arias by someone else—no problem—in they went. Viewed in the most
positive light, the very process of composition was a sort of open and
ongoing collaboration, made easier by a shared stylistic vocabulary that
allowed composers and artists to mix and match preexisting musical
materials at will. Seen in this context, any reservations about Handel's
borrowing habits seem far less significant than they otherwise might.

We also need to distinguish between borrowing and the modern
notion of "copyright," which is a term of legal art designed to protect the
ownership rights, and therefore the income, of an author in his work.
In Handel's day such a thing did not exist. Rights in a work were often
owned, not by its author, but by the publisher who took the financial

risk in printing the sheet music, and no group was more unscrupulous in this regard. To protect his rights, Handel either had to publish and sell his own work, or make a deal with an existing firm to issue authorized versions of his most popular or newest pieces.

The deeper question when it comes to Handel's borrowings, however, is an aesthetic one, and concerns whether he deserves credit as a creator of *original* work. In this respect I have to be dogmatic. Originality, in the modern sense of "uniqueness," is overrated. Much of the greatest music ever written has been based on borrowed material. The entire sacred repertoire, from the origins of polyphony in the late medieval period right up to the baroque at the start of the seventeenth century, consists almost entirely of music based either on Gregorian chant or secular song. Take away all of Bach's music built on Lutheran chorale melodies, and his repertoire of sacred music (that is, most of what he wrote) vanishes almost completely.

Handel received very thorough early training as a German church musician, just as Bach did, but what sets him apart is the fact that he took what might be viewed as an unexceptional practice when applied to the composition of, say, a church cantata, and applied it wholesale to the very secular fields of opera, oratorio, and instrumental music. Moreover, he did it with abandon, grabbing stuff from just about anywhere and using it however he pleased. He was music's first great eclectic, making no effort and seeing no need to hide his technique, driven only by his concern to use the right material in the most effective context. Audiences in his day, to the extent they may have noticed at all, for the most part didn't care, because the result, wherever it came from, always sounded personal and fresh.

For example, Handel was a very great melodist. Some composers dream up tunes anew, while others assemble them from smaller, found musical objects. Handel did both, but he was a particularly supreme virtuoso at piecing ready-made ideas together, which is probably related to the art of improvising at the keyboard. In our own time, the composer Francis Poulenc wrote music similarly, blending classical clichés and Parisian street music with truly disconcerting seamlessness. Handel never displays Poulenc's slapstick intentions, but he achieves the same naturalness and fluidity of line. Later critics accused Handel of trying to cover his tracks—not because that is what he actually did, but because the music itself does it so supremely well.

The work that initially had the musical world so agitated about the issue of borrowing was *Israel in Egypt* (1739) when, in the latter half of the nineteenth century, it became clear that Handel had adapted large chunks of earlier sacred and secular music by Italian composers Alessandro Stradella, Francesco Urio, and Dionigi Erba (the technical term for this technique of setting new text to preexisting music is *parody*). The first two of these composers were long dead by the time Handel wrote his oratorio; Erba's dates remain uncertain to this day. Suffice it say that the Victorian musical world was not amused to discover that a "sacred" classic based entirely on words from Scripture was not completely original work, presumably uniquely inspired by the Holy Spirit.

Ironically, the only reason we know or talk about these earlier composers (and more than a few others) today is because Handel thought highly enough of them to appropriate some of their work. Absent his involvement their obscurity would be almost absolute. After all, you don't see recordings and baroque music festivals dedicated to Erba and Urio popping up anywhere based on their own merits. Stradella is a different story, but not significantly so as regards the Handel connection. The largest borrowing in *Israel* in fact comes from its own composer: Handel's *Funeral Anthem for Queen Caroline* "The ways of Zion do mourn" (1737), in its entirety, became the oratorio's original part 1.

For modern listeners, Handel's omnivorous compositional technique proves to be an unalloyed blessing. The reason, as just suggested, is because the most popular and frequently accessed source of Handel's borrowings is Handel himself. This means that his output, no matter how diverse his sources or broad his range of expression, forms a consistent musical language unified by recurring ideas, gestures, phrases, motives, and other aural signposts. It is delightful and so very satisfying to encounter a new work, recognize a familiar idea, and be able to say, "Aha! That is Handel." And the more you listen, the more your recognition of Handel's proprietary musical vocabulary increases, and the more entertaining the experience becomes.

To illustrate how helpful Handel's borrowings and stylistic signposts can be, let me take you through some of the samples that come with this book track by track, both to see what he absorbed and adapted, and explore how this knowledge can be used as a means of moving easily from a work that you do know, to another awaiting discovery.

Track 1. "Eternal source of light divine" (*Ode for the Birthday of Queen Anne*)

Between 1717 and 1719, Handel worked as house composer at the Cannons estate of James Brydges, Earl of Carnarvon, and later First Duke of Chandos. Brydges maintained a private orchestra plus a small group of singers, and for this establishment Handel wrote what have come down to us as the Chandos Anthems—eleven sacred pieces based on psalm texts. We discussed them briefly in the last chapter. Like so many of the early cantatas, these works became useful source material for much that followed, and Handel raided them freely; but they also absorbed a good bit of his earlier music as well.

Anthem No. 11, *Let God Arise*, contains a brief chorus setting the text "Praised be the Lord," which pretty clearly comes from the same conceptual territory as "Eternal source of light divine" from the *Ode for the Birthday of Queen Anne*. The melodies aren't exactly the same, but the rhythms, textures, and harmonic treatment all recall the earlier work, with divided high and low choral voices taking the place of countertenor and trumpet in the original. Generally when we think of borrowing we imagine someone stealing "the tune," but the range of ideas in music is much larger than that, and here's a case in point.

Track 2. "Dominus a dextris tuis" (*Dixit Dominus*)

As you may recall, the text of this psalm deals with God doing a lot of very graphic smiting, and so it should come as no surprise that Handel found that music appropriate to the opening chorus of the same Chandos Anthem just mentioned. There, the words are:

> Let God arise, and let His enemies be scatter'd;
> Let them also that hate Him, flee before Him.

As is almost invariably the case, the musical quotation isn't literal, if only because the music had to be adapted to a new text, but the derivation is perfectly obvious nonetheless. You hear the same falling phrases at "let His enemies be scatter'd" that we heard previously to illustrate "implebit ruinas" (plus some extra virtuoso coloratura to illustrate the "scattering"), while the same war chant that characterized "conquassabit capita in terra multorum" now illustrates the panicked retreat of God's enemies.

Let God Arise is in fact a particularly bountiful work for Handel detectives. The musical texture of its final chorus, "Blessed be God. Alleluia," was absorbed into the "Hallelujah Chorus" at the words "For the Lord God omnipotent reigneth," so you might say that this particular piece giveth as much as it taketh.

Track 3. "Disserratevi, o porte d'Averno" (*La Resurrezione*)

The instrumental introduction, or ritornello, of an aria usually comes to a full close, which is convenient since you're most likely going to hear it again at the very end to wrap up the proceedings. Bits of it also appear between vocal episodes, and any amount of it may form part of the sung melody. The brilliant ritornello from "Disserratevi" is a self-contained piece all by itself, even if it's quite short, and so when Handel needed an energetic introduction to the alto aria "Mighty love now calls to arm" in his oratorio *Alexander Balus* (1747), he turned to the forty-year-old opening number of his second major Italian-language oratorio.

Comparison between the two is fascinating. The earlier aria is a traditional ABA, very formal in shape. "Mighty love," on the other hand, is two minutes and thirty seconds of vocal fireworks without the standard "B" section. Handel works in bits of the ritornello in both cases, but the earlier piece draws a sharper distinction between the vocal and orchestral parts, whereas the English oratorio version—with an entirely different vocal line—features whiplash exchanges between the singer, oboes, and trumpets. Both are tremendously exciting, and extremely challenging for the singer, but the overall effect is quite different in context: a dazzling introductory showpiece versus a short, punchy, dramatic interlude.

Incidentally, I don't recommend that you spend a big chunk of change getting a recording of *Alexander Balus* unless the entire piece interests you. Like so many of Handel's less well-known works, it has only been recorded a couple of times, and the best complete set (Robert King on Hyperion) will run you about $30. The piece has a lot going for it, but for our purposes here you can easily download the individual track for pennies and that's all you need to do if you're curious about making this particular comparison.

Track 4. "Ogni vento" (Agrippina)

Handel's opera *Agrippina* premiered with great success in Venice in 1709. It marks the culmination of his Italian period, and contains almost no original music. The vast majority of it consists of material borrowed from his earlier Italian works, including this deliciously fresh and breezy aria, which began life as "Bella fiamma" ("Beautiful flame") in the cantata *Aminta e Fillide* (a.k.a. *Arresta il passo*, or "Stop!"). As in the previously discussed "Da tempeste il legno infranto," this is a simile aria about a ship being steered safely into port—a very popular image back in the day, evidently. Here is the full text:

> Ogni vento ch'al porto lo spinga,
> ben che fiero minacci tempeste,
> l'ampie vele gli spande il nocchier.
>
> Regni il figlio, mia sola lusinga,
> sian le stelle in aspetto funeste,
> senza pena le guarda il pensier.
>
> Every wind that blows into port,
> Which proudly threatens a tempest,
> Challenges the steersman in full sail.

> My son will reign, my only wish,
> May the fateful stars,
> Watch over my plans without pity.

In the opera, as we have already mentioned, Agrippina is scheming to get her son Nero installed as emperor of Rome. As it seems she's finally on the verge of success (having plotted to have everyone else murdered), she expresses relief that her devious plans are finally coming to fruition. The reason that Handel can transfer the aria so easily from cantata to opera is that, as with "Da tempeste," the music does not indulge in literal illustration of the text as much as it embodies the psychological state of the singer, and this is much the same in both cases.

The ritornello of this aria is extraordinary. It is a catchy sort of merry-go-round waltz, with unexpected phrase-lengths that give the piece a wonderful, lilting quality. Current scholarship asserts that the melodic bits that make up the main tune originated in operas by Handel's elder Hamburg colleague Reinhard Keiser (1674–1739). This may be true, but the art here is in the arrangement; the various thematic bits also have a timeless, folksy quality that suggest that they may in turn have come from some earlier, musical public domain, with Keiser representing one way-station among many. Handel again reused just the first phrase of the melody for the song "Happy Beauty" in the English language version of his oratorio *The Triumph of Time and Truth*, whereas the merry-go-round waltz music turned up, in different rhythm but still recognizable, as part of the aria "È un incendio frà due venti" ("Like a fire between two winds") in *Rinaldo*. The aria (and later chorus) "To song and dance we give the day," from *Samson*, makes no direct thematic reference but clearly belongs to the same family of ideas.

Aside from *Agrippina*, an opera that every Handel lover should own, the cantata *Aminta e Fillide* is well worth having, too, and not just to compare the two versions of this same aria. The cantata contains, among other gems, the first version, "Se vago rio," of the haunting, exotic melody that later became the mermaid's song "Il vostro maggio" in *Rinaldo*. It has been splendidly recorded on the Glossa label, with first-class singers directed by Fabio Bonizzoni, as part of the series of discs devoted to Handel's Italian cantatas with instrumental accompaniment.

Track 5. "Ombra mai fù" (Serse)

Handel's setting has already been discussed in chapter 1, but as a source of alleged borrowing the story is far from over. One of his London rivals was Italian composer Giovanni Bononcini. The two (along with Filippo Amadei) actually collaborated on an opera produced in 1721 called *Muzio Scevola*. Handel wrote the third act; Bononcini, the second. Much earlier, in 1694, Bononcini had written his own opera *Xerse*, to the same libretto as Handel did later. Some modern scholarship alleges that elements of Handel's setting of "Ombra mai fù" owe a debt to Bononcini, and it does seem that their rivalry stimulated Handel to a certain amount of competitive borrowing, possibly in order to show "how it ought to be done." If so, then the point would not have been to disguise the derivation at all, but just the opposite: to challenge the audience to make the comparison.

That said, I have seen Bononcini's version of "Ombra mai fù," and sure enough, the two are almost identical—except for such minor details as length, tempo designation, melody, harmony, text setting— in other words, who are we kidding? They have practically nothing in common except a certain similarity of mood inevitably produced by the fact that both composers are telling the same story. Indeed, many allegations of thievery by Handel turn out to be classic examples of the logical fallacy know in Latin as *post hoc, ergo propter hoc*, which means "after this, therefore the result of this." In other words, just because something comes first, whatever follows later, even if similar, is not necessarily causally related.

However, Bononcini himself was the object of a genuine plagiarism scandal when it turned out that he had stolen a madrigal by Antonio Lotti, passing it off as his own work for performance in London. Unfortunately for Bononcini, Lotti (1667–1740) was alive and kicking and able to substantiate his claim. Note the difference between this fact pattern and Handel's practice. Bononcini stole an entire piece and claimed original authorship; Handel always *adapted* what he used in some way or another, even if only to change the text, the scoring, or the larger context. Adaptation, it seems, was acceptable; flagrant thievery of whole works, especially from a living composer, was not.

Track 6. "Se tanto piace al cor" (*Ariodante*)

In this aria, the lovelorn Dalinda sings wistfully of her hope that she will ultimately win her evil boyfriend Polinesso's affection. All of the music is original; it is the rhythm that Handel has borrowed, or rather, employed as part of his era's common practice. The piece is a siciliano (or siciliana), a graceful dance with gently rocking rhythm, usually notated in compound time (6/8 or 12/8). If this sounds technical, don't worry. You know what a siciliano sounds like. "Greensleeves" is one; so is the Christmas carol "Silent Night."

Indeed, a great deal of Christmas music uses siciliano rhythms, including the "Pifa" or "Pastoral Symphony" in Handel's *Messiah*. This is because of a very long-standing association of this dance with music of folklike or rural character, and also (in slower tempos), with lullabies. One popular variant of "Rockabye Baby" is a siciliano. So are "Dolce bene" in *Radamisto*, "Se 'l mio duol" from *Rodelinda*, "Credete al mio dolore" from *Alcina*, "Your charms to ruin led the way" in *Samson*, and the chorus "Ye sons of Israel, mourn" in *Esther*. The siciliano aria "Se vago rio," just mentioned, not only reappears as the Mermaid's Song in *Rinaldo*, but it ultimately morphed into the tenor aria "Let me wander not unseen," specifically marked "Siciliana" in the pastoral ode *L'Allegro, il Penseroso ed il Moderato*. Handel was a master of this style, both for music evoking the countryside or the natural world, and for the expression of wistful or pathetic longing and grief in minor keys.

Here, then, is the text of Dalinda's aria "Se tanto piace al cor," a typical example of Handel's expressively compelling way with the siciliano, and an exquisite melody by any standard:

> Se tanto piace al cor
> il volto tuo Signor
> quando disprezzi,
> al cor quanto sarà
> cara la tua beltà,
> quando accarezzi.

> If your face, Sir, pleases my heart so much when you scorn me,
> Then my heart will cherish your handsome looks even more
> when you caress me.

Note: you can find "Se vago rio" on the same excellent Harmonia Mundi disc by Lucy Crowe that contains the version of "Disserratevi" included in the sample tracks.

Track 7. Concerto Grosso Op. 6, No. I

Handel's instrumental works, as we have seen, participated in his borrowing binge as fervently as the vocal pieces—indeed, perhaps more so. For much of the eighteenth century the line between, say, a chamber work and an orchestral one could be blurry simply because music was written for a specific number of parts, or "voices," with no limit on how many players you could assign to a musical line. This made it very easy to switch between media and it encouraged composers to reuse individual movements on different occasions. This work offers a case in point.

Originally scored for strings when first published in 1739, Handel's Concerti Grossi Op. 6 also served as interlude music between the acts of his oratorios, where he had the opportunity to add oboe parts. Individual movements also could be adapted as needed, and so the first movement of this concerto found a spot as a "symphony" in act 2 of *The Occasional Oratorio*. The lovely, serene Musette that follows in the choral work also stopped by for a visit from its original home in the middle of Concerto Grosso No. 6.

The concerto's finale, on the other hand, shares material with Scarlatti's Keyboard Sonata in G Major, K. 2, which had just been published in London when Handel wrote his concertos. Both pieces start with the same motive, but the ensuing treatment is quite individual, with Scarlatti moving quickly into a minor key and Handel indulging his usual love of rhythmic quirks and unpredictable phrasing. You can find recordings of the Scarlatti for download pretty easily, including a famous version on piano by the late, great Clara Haskil.

Often, in considering Handel's borrowings from other composers, you will find him tickled by just a handful of notes, or a short motive, and this sets him off on his own subsequent journey. Another good example of this from orchestral music is the "symphony" following "Call all my wise men" in the oratorio *Belshazzar*. The clear intent here is to provide a sense of time passing as, in an actual staging, would be necessary to gather the wise men and bring them before the king. For the music Handel turned to his longtime friend Georg Philipp Telemann, and the "Postillons" from his *Tafelmusik* ("Table Music"), a vivacious piece that features the call of a post-horn.

Handel only borrowed the initial horn call; the rest of the piece is his own. It could be that the borrowed bit was a generic signal that audiences of the day might have known, or perhaps it just struck him as the right thing in the right place. Either way, short musical interludes—military marches, fanfares, dance numbers, and many other, similar items—must have been part of the common currency of the period, and the only thing that prevents us from knowing for sure is our unfamiliarity with the vast range of music from daily life that was so normal that it had no known author and no need to be discussed.

Track 8. "Fammi combattere" (*Orlando*)

"Fammi combattere" belongs to the heroic category of aria. These pieces abound with flashy coloratura, striking orchestral gestures, trumpet fanfares, and other warlike imagery. The main themes are also usually simple, unsubtle, and stubbornly memorable. Handel in heroic mode often finds motives that fit the words so well that seem bound together in a sort of indissoluble union—how interesting, then, that this aria starts with music amazingly similar to "Let the bright seraphim," the equally flashy and inevitable-sounding closing number of the oratorio *Samson*. And once again we note that Handel makes no purposeful distinction between sacred and secular subjects; his sole concern is truthfulness and accuracy of expression.

As you can see from the text and translation below, Orlando is surely nuts. His insanity in this and many other "Orlando" operas is often portrayed as more comic than tragic.

> Fammi combattere
> mostri e tifei,
> nuovi trofei
> se vuoi dal mio valor.

Muraglie abbattere
disfar incanti,
se vuoi ch'io vanti
darti prove d'amor.

Let me fight every monster if you want new trophies of my valor.
Beat down walls, destroy spells,
If you want me to brag about giving you proof of love.

"Let the bright seraphim," by the way, is popular as a recital number, and you can hear a spectacular performance of it sung by soprano Sandrine Piau on an aria recital disc *Between Heaven and Earth* (Naïve). Of course, *Samson* is also one of Handel's greatest oratorios—much as I hate to say it, because you can see how quickly the hours are starting to pile up (*Samson* plays for a whopping three and a half) and I am keenly aware of the fact that we only have so much available time in the day. It's a true embarrassment of riches.

Track 10. "Lascia ch'io pianga" (*Rinaldo*)

This, one of Handel's most beautiful arias from perhaps his most popular opera in modern times (when superstar mezzo-soprano Cecilia Bartoli makes a complete recording then you know we're getting somewhere), has a fascinating history. It began life, apparently, as an instrumental sarabande (a type of slow dance) in the first act of Handel's first opera, *Almira* (1705), from his Hamburg period. He was only nineteen. The similarity is more rhythmic than melodic, and we have to be careful in drawing conclusions. Virtually the exact same pattern (and even the melody, in part) characterizes the charming Prelude in C Major from Shostakovich's 24 Preludes and Fugues for piano, Op. 87, and that in turn sounds like a transcription of an episode from the finale of the same composer's "Leningrad" Symphony (No. 7).

We have no evidence that Handel was thinking of that sarabande when he wrote the aria "Lascia la spina" ("Leave the thorn") two years later for the 1707 premiere of his first Italian oratorio, *Il trionfo del Tempo e del Disinganno*. We also don't know whether Handel was the original author of the piece found in *Almira*. It's that generic. I suspect he would have viewed the aria as a completely new and independent piece, and not as a "development" or "arrangement" of the sarabande. As it stands, all we know for sure is that during the intervening period a relatively uninteresting, throwaway dance number became one of the most heartfelt expressions of sorrow in the entire operatic literature, even if it hadn't quite found its ultimate home yet. That had to wait until 1711, and the premiere of *Rinaldo*, the first Italian opera written especially for an English audience.

Musically, the two versions of the aria are quite similar as regards the main theme. The principal differences lay in Handel's decision to cut the initial orchestral statement of the ritornello in the *Rinaldo* version and start right off with the voice, as well as the substantially rewritten "B" section later on. These changes tighten up the structure and better suit a work designed for actual staging, as opposed to concert performance in an aristocratic home (however large or elaborate the room), but otherwise there is little to choose between the two arrangements. Handel knew a good thing when he heard it.

> Lascia ch'io pianga
> Mia cruda sorte,
> E che sospiri
> La libertà.
>
> Il duolo infranga
> Queste ritorte,
> De' miei martiri
> Sol per pietà.
>
> Let me weep
> For my cruel fate,
> And I sigh
> For freedom.
>
> Suffering should break
> These chains
> Of my martyrdom
> Mercifully.

In the years following the premiere of *Rinaldo*, "Lascia ch'io pianga" became so popular that when Handel revived *Il trionfo del Tempo e del Disinganno*, first in an extended version in the 1730s and later, in English, at the very end of his life, he composed a new, perky version of "Lascia la spina." It works for an interesting reason. While the original text also speaks of sorrow, its message is a warning to avoid it. Handel thus has a choice: he can illustrate the object of the warning, or the result of advice taken (that is, happiness). The quick second version adopts this alternative viewpoint. Handel used it again in the pasticcio *Giove in Argo*. Both "Lascia la spina" and "Lascia ch'io pianga" are extremely popular concert items, and aside from the lovely version included here you may well find performances piling up as you collect Handel recitals, never mind recordings of the two larger works from which they come.

Track 11. "Sibilar l'angui d'Aletto" (*Aci, Galatea e Polifemo*)

This one's easy. Polifemo is a bad guy. Argante in *Rinaldo* is a bad guy. So Handel just took the aria from the 1708 serenata and stuck it into the 1711 opera. The words are really juicy, as long as you know your Greek mythology (Alecto is one of the furies; Scylla, a monster with several slathering dog heads):

> Sibillar gli angui d'Aletto,
> E latrar vorace Scilla,
> Parmi udir d'intorno a me.
>
> Rio velen mi serpe in petto,
> Né ancor languida favilla
> Di timor, pena mi diè.
>
> The hissing of Alecto's snakes,
> Scylla's hungry barking,
> I hear surround me.

Evil venom writhes in my breast,
Not even the lazy spark
Of fear, gives me pause.

Handel had a much larger orchestra at his disposal for the operatic version of this aria, and he takes full advantage of the extra strings, trumpets, and timpani. Contrary to what the words seem to suggest, the music itself is not in any way scary or threatening. Rather, this is music in the "heroic" style, an expression of pride and a boastful assertion of courage—a character's self-satisfied confidence in his own badness. The vocal range and dexterity required for this aria verge on the superhuman, especially for the bass voice, which, like any heavy object, tends to move less quickly and more awkwardly than the lighter and higher categories. Prior to the baroque revival of the past few decades and the advent of property trained soloists, this piece would have been considered all but unsingable.

Track 14. "Rejoice, O Judah! Hallelujah! Amen" (*Judas Maccabaeus*)

We conclude with Handel in "Hallelujah" mode. The issue here is not one of borrowing, but rather his frequent recourse to a style of which he was the inventor and greatest exponent. Music is full of iconic personal fingerprints: the "Rossini crescendo," the "Mozart rhythm," or the special endings that we already discussed in the Introduction. Handel wrote dozens of "Hallelujahs," "Alleluias" and "Amens." While no two are precisely identical, they are all supremely theatrical, exciting, and they sound like no one else.

Here Handel begins with a bass solo; this becomes a chorus, and then the orchestration increases in density until the trumpets and drums enter and the entire ensemble reaches the apex of Handelian brilliance. The advantage to dealing with "Hallelujah," "Amen," or some variant of these, is that they are basically nonsense words that can be repeated ad infinitum, permitting the composer to focus on building a purely musical climax. Master of sonority and texture that he was, Handel never fails to thrill at these moments, and the secret of his effectiveness lies in the unashamed simplicity and honesty of the conception.

If there is any lesson to be learned from consideration of Handel's habit of borrowing, either from himself or others, it is this: in terms of musical quality it makes absolutely no difference. We cannot know what induced him to write new music in some instances, and resort to adaptations in others, but anyone who insists that works containing more original material are inherently better is making a value judgment that has nothing to do with the real world experience of listening. There is no evidence at all that Handel's compositional choices resulted from laziness, lack of inspiration, or pressure of time. *Israel in Egypt* was a masterpiece of Handelian workmanship before we knew where some of its material came from, and it remains one now that we do know.

Notes

Preface

1. Recordings of large works are identified by conductor and label. For recitals, you only need the name of the soloist and the label. This is the bare minimum necessary to locate a given title efficiently.
2. William Coxe: *Anecdotes of George Frederick Handel and John Christopher Smith* (London: Tiger of the Stripe, 2009), 39.

Chapter 1

3. *Due cori* means "two choirs," and in Handel's orchestral works this means the opposition of the main body of strings to two independent groups of wind instruments, consisting primarily of oboes and horns.
4. As always in describing Handel's scoring, and unlike later music, the numerical quantity of woodwinds refers to parts, not instruments. The actual number of players per part can be multiplied at will depending on the size the string section.
5. "No, you do not trust me," "Which flower laughs at dawn," and "If you do not let love."
6. *Messiah* otherwise calls for five vocal soloists (in most versions), five-part chorus, two oboes, two trumpets, strings, timpani, and continuo (with harpsichord and organ).

Chapter 2

7. Which is indeed the title of Saint-Saëns's last opera (premiered in 1911) on the same story.

Chapter 4

8. A brief word on language and translations: I do like to provide them where it's most helpful, but there are some listeners to like to follow the text word by word, and others who prefer just to get the gist of what's going on and then sit back and enjoy the music. I do both. Neither is better or "right," and it's entirely a matter of personal preference or mood. So, I offer both methods throughout this book, as should be clear by this point. The synopsis of *Ariodante* employs the "summary" method simply to keep it brief. The entire libretto is available online, and translations of major arias are generally easy to find.

9. The information comes mostly from Dean, supplemented by my own review of the scores and reference to the lists of players in the recommended recordings.

10. Christopher Hogwood, *Handel* (New York: Thames & Hudson, 2007), 282–83.

Chapter 6

11. For performance, the number of instruments indicates the number of parts, not the number of players per line, in keeping with baroque practice. The string parts could be (and should be) multiplied unless otherwise indicated. Wind parts may be doubled. "Bass" usually means cellos, basses, and possibly bassoon, along with the usual continuo instruments (harpsichord and possibly lute/theorbo).

12. Most arias are preceded by a secco recitative.

13. So called for clarity, to distinguish the voice from the instrumental bass.

14. There is also an earlier setting of this same text, for soprano solo, HWV236, which dates from Handel's pre-Italian, Hamburg period.

CD Track Listing

1. "Eternal source of light divine" (*Ode for the Birthday of Queen Anne*) 3:01
   Andreas Scholl, countertenor
   Akademie für Alte Musik Berlin, Marcus Creed (cond.)
   Harmonia Mundi HMC 902041

2. Dominus a dextris tuis (Dixit Dominus) 6:18
   Soloists; Vocalconsort Berlin; Akademie für Alte Musik Berlin, Marcus Creed (cond.)
   Harmonia Mundi HMC 902041

3. "Disserratevi, o porte d'Averno" (*La Resurrezione*) 5:25
   Lucy Crowe (soprano)
   The English Concert, Harry Bicket (cond.)
   HMU 907559

4. "Ogni vento" (*Agrippina*) 5:18
   Lorraine Hunt (mezzo-soprano)
   Philharmonia Baroque Orchestra, Nicholas McGegan (cond.)
   HMU 907056

5. "Ombra mai fù" (*Serse*) 3:00
   Andreas Scholl (countertenor)
   Akademie für Alte Musik Berlin
   HMC 901685

6. "Se tanto piace al cor" (*Ariodante*) 3:50
   Lisa Saffer (soprano)
   Freiburger Barockorchester, Nicholas McGegan (cond.)
   HMU 907146.68

7. Concerto Grosso Op. 6, No. 1 11:07
    The Academy of Ancient Music, Andrew Manze (cond.)
    HMU 907228.29

8. "Fammi combattere" (*Orlando*) 3:54
    Bejun Mehta (countertenor)
    Freiburger Barockorchester, René Jacobs (cond.)
    HMC 902077

9. Symphony, Recitative, and Chorus: "Welcome, welcome, mighty king!" (*Saul*) 2:47
    Rosemary Joshua (soprano); RIAS Kammerchor; Concerto Köln, René Jacobs (cond.)
    HMY 2921877.78

10. "Lascia ch'io pianga" (*Rinaldo*) 6:10
    Miah Persson (soprano)
    Freiburger Barockorchester, René Jacobs (cond.)
    HMY 2921796.98

11. "Sibilar l'angui d'Aletto" (*Aci, Galatea e Polifemo*) 4:12
    David Thomas (bass)
    London Baroque, Charles Medlam (cond.)
    HMC 901253.54

12. "Se pietà di me non senti" (*Giulio Cesare*) 10:49
    Lisa Saffer (soprano)
    Philharmonia Baroque Orchestra, Nicholas McGegan (cond.)
    HMU 907036

13. "Da tempeste il legno infranto" (*Giulio Cesare*) 6:14
    Lisa Saffer (soprano)
    Philharmonia Baroque Orchestra, Nicholas McGegan (cond.)
    HMU 907036

14. "Rejoice, O Judah! Hallelujah! Amen" (*Judas Maccabaeus*) 3:17
    David Thomas (bass); U.C. Berkeley Chamber Chorus; Philharmonia Baroque Orchestra, Nicholas McGegan (cond.)
    HMX 2907374.75